The authors of Educere *hav*
that will both inspire and eq
forward in a manner that is s........... *, ... design principles*
and educational research. It is an essential resource for all leaders committed
to improving the quality of our schools.

— Wendy J. Harris, Q.C.
Education Law Specialist
Harris & Company LLP

Educere *is a roadmap to quality educational reform. Rather than presenting*
a superficial, cookie-cutter approach to systems development, the authors
provide guidance for enacting lasting change, leading to enhanced outcomes
for students. They take research and connect it to the heart of teaching.
Moreover, they do it in a way that is engaging and is informed by their
extensive experience. District administrators who pick it up will find
themselves consulting it on a regular basis.

— Kent McIntosh, Ph.D.
College of Education
University of Oregon

Educere *is a powerful and transformative book. The synthesis of educational*
philosophy and practical leadership understandings provides district and
school-based leaders with a comprehensive framework for action towards
meaningful change.

— Brad Bauman
Director of Instruction – Education Services
Surrey School District

EDUCERE

*System Design and Development
for Public Schooling*

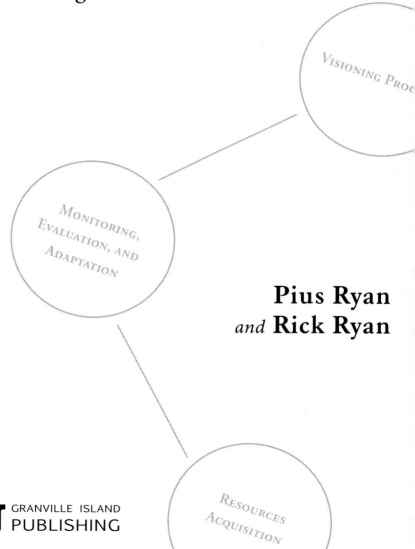

VISIONING PROC

MONITORING,
EVALUATION, AND
ADAPTATION

RESOURCES
ACQUISITION

Pius Ryan
and **Rick Ryan**

GRANVILLE ISLAND
PUBLISHING

Library and Archives Canada Cataloguing in Publication

Ryan, Pius
    Educere : system design and development for public schooling / Pius Ryan and Rick Ryan.

Includes bibliographical references.
ISBN 978-1-926991-21-4

    1. Instructional systems—Design. 2. Public schools. I. Ryan, Rick II. Title.

LB1028.38.R92 2012   371.33   C2012-904798-8

Editors: Lisa Ferdman and Brooke Kosty
Proofreader: Kyle Hawke
Cover designer: Alisha Whitley
Text and graphics designer: Omar Gallegos

Granville Island Publishing Ltd.
212–1656 Duranleau St.
Vancouver, BC, Canada V6H 3S4
604-688-0320 / 1-877-688-0320
www.granvilleislandpublishing.com

Printed in Canada on recycled paper

Why the title *Educere*? The word *education* is derived from its Latin root, *educare*, which, in turn, can be traced to the Latin root words *e* and *ducere*. Thus, *educere* means "to lead out."

Adaequatio intellectus et rei

Contents

Acknowledgements

We would like to convey our sincere gratitude to the many individuals who have guided us throughout our lives and have influenced us in more ways than they know. They also have inspired us to reflect upon profound questions, some of which are included in this book. In particular, we would like to thank Alex Marshall for his faith and friendship, and Gary Smith, mentor and friend.

Thank you, also, to our publisher, Jo Blackmore, for her guidance in this process and for the management of her excellent team. A special thank you to Lisa Ferdman for her comprehensive revision of the manuscript and for her relentless attention to detail, and to Brooke Kosty for her extensive work with structure and for making our concepts more accessible. Thank you, also, to Omar Gallegos for his expert design of text and graphics, to Alisha Whitley for her striking cover design, and to Kyle Hawke for his diligent attention to the text and design.

Our deepest affection and gratitude go to our wives, for their unfailing support throughout our writing of this book. And our love for our children spurs us to offer them the best education possible.

Foreword

The expectations and demands placed upon public-school education in the twenty-first century are unprecedented. In today's Western societies, public schools are entrusted with the task of imparting to our youth the core skills and specialized knowledge that will enable them to succeed in an increasingly challenging world. Moreover, these institutions are now being held accountable for student outcomes; established standards are required to be met in order to ensure that the next generation of citizens will contribute to a vibrant social and economic future.

How have we adapted our school systems to enhance the learning process in accordance with students' needs and with our latest understanding of cognitive development? Few educational systems garner high marks in devising an architecture that connects current awareness with best practice. Yet many school systems are awakening to the realities and exigencies of twenty-first-century education.

Learning organizations are urged to adopt a coherent vision and strategy that embrace crucial changes in teaching and learning dynamics. Board of Education governors and senior staff members have observed that successful school systems follow the three essential principles of a quality organization: alignment, coherence, and sustainability.

District and school leaders are encouraged to jettison outdated educational methodologies, to disrupt predictability and the status quo, and to generate a collaborative plan for school improvement. Traditional leadership traits such as charisma, resolve, courage, and certainty no longer suffice in guiding an organization. An effective leader must construct networks in which authority is intentionally subordinate to relevant expertise. Leaders who confront ambiguity and uncertainty cultivate a humility and relentlessness that prove invaluable assets.

Education is justifiably regarded as a sacred calling, and leadership as a journey of discovery. Our vision, dedication, wisdom, expertise, and integrity all must be employed in generating the best possible outcomes for our students. They are entitled to nothing less.

Mike McKay
Superintendent of Schools and CEO
Surrey School District

Preface

The Need for a New Approach
to Public Schooling

"Write down the thoughts of the moment. Those that come unsought for are commonly the most valuable."

— Francis Bacon

Throughout our careers in education, we have engaged in countless conversations addressing various critical issues:

- the historical and philosophical roots of public schooling

- the lack of clarity regarding the role and appropriate limits of public schooling

- the ever-increasing expectations placed upon public schooling

- the confusion engendered by continual, and sometimes contradictory, innovations or proposed practices

- the need for change, while maintaining focus upon the development of quality schools

- the limited use of key research in implementing improvements

- the preliminary understandings regarding organizational design principles

- the lack of sustained and targeted professional development, which is critical for system-wide improvement

- the need for system-wide improvement, to facilitate learning in today's increasingly complex classroom environments

These conversations impelled us to share, in writing, the practical design strategies for system development that we have implemented successfully in our district over the last several years.

This work is not intended to be exhaustive in its discussion of leadership and organizational-theory elements such as management, communication, and quality assurance. Instead, we have incorporated the ideas of recognized thinkers on these subjects in developing our action plan. The resulting practical resource tools will assist policy-makers, superintendents, directors, and principals in forging a dynamic learning environment.

While we are keenly aware that there are no simple, prescriptive answers or checklist approaches to authentic system development, we offer a far-reaching conceptual perspective and suggestions that may readily be implemented. At its core, enduring organizational change requires collective inquiry and a profound commitment to improvement.

Chapter 1

The Role of Public Schooling: From Its Roots to the Present

"Education is not preparation for life; education is life itself."

— John Dewey

Universal public schooling is a relatively recent enterprise, the result of the need for a more educated citizenry. Yet we can offer an excellent education that also enables students to advance society's goals only if we recognize modern public schooling's historical roots. The development of public education has been informed largely by Aristotle's interrelated forms of knowledge: 1) *episteme* (analytical reason); 2) *techne* (technical reason, or craft; i.e., artistic productivity); and 3) *phronesis* (ethical deliberation, or practical wisdom).

Modern Western education has evolved around the aims of individual development and socialization, and the acquisition of knowledge. The policy statements of every Canadian province reflect a consensus that public schools should promote the following: 1) individual development; 2) socialization; 3) vocational preparation; and 4) economic good. More specifically, the *British Columbia School Act* states that an educational program consists of:

3

> ... an organized set of learning activities that ... is
> designed to enable learners to develop their indivi-
> dual potential and to acquire the knowledge, skills
> and attitudes needed to contribute to a healthy,
> democratic and pluralistic society and a prosperous and
> sustainable economy.

Recently, there has been a demand for public-school accountability
with regard to student outcomes. The new hyper-focus upon success,
as measured by literacy, numeracy, and social-responsibility standards,
seems to allow public schooling little room to function as more than
a means to simplistic, measurable ends. The historical notion of the
well-educated individual, whose intellectual, aesthetic, psychological,
and spiritual traits were well integrated, has evidently been supplanted
by the idea that students are required merely to master particular
skills, thus enabling them to perform efficiently in a competitive
environment. This is deeply troubling.

A well-rounded education is, to a significant degree, the mediating
influence on the path from ignorance to reason. Some four hundred
years ago, Francis Bacon wrote about the importance of reason, noting
that the cultivation of the ability to reason is essential to an educated
citizenry and to a purposeful society. He asserted that, in the absence
of reason, we are left with unfounded and illogical decisions:

> ... The human understanding when it has once adopted
> an opinion ... draws all things else to support and agree
> with it. And though there be a greater number and
> weight of instances to be found on the other side, yet
> these it either neglects and despises, or else by some
> distinction sets aside and rejects.

Many educational commentators contend that the recent shift in society's expectations of education, and the current clamour for accountability, have been precipitated by a general loss of confidence in public schooling. Darrell Bricker and Edward Greenspon, in their book *Searching for Certainty: Inside the Canadian Mindset*, maintain that:

> ... the real public opinion story in education is more about changed expectations than decay in the system ... Growing expectations were responsible for the cratering in the early 1990s of confidence in the system. Confidence in all institutions in our society suffered significant reversals in the early part of the decade in part because of the overall decline in deference in all Western societies ... but education fell faster and harder than any other institution.

However, any higher ideals regarding public schooling may unintentionally be *impeded* by the agenda of accountability. The demand for accountability originated as a reassuring, precautionary measure to instill public confidence in an educational system with which the larger community had become disillusioned. Thus, accountability actually serves a political purpose. Bricker and Greenspon state:

> ... One of the most striking findings in our research is the overwhelming level of support for student and teacher testing. The time is well past when parents accept[ed] as an article of faith that their children were on the receiving end of a good education and that teachers and schools were equipping them for the challenges of the future. The decline in public trust and

the concurrent drift of schools from social institutions to economic institutions has ushered in an evidence-based, show-me age. Parents are insisting upon independent, objective, and measurable information. Without transparency, there cannot be accountability. And without accountability, the search for certainty is futile.

Unfortunately, this new reality enables those outside the educational system to determine important aspects of its agenda. The assessment and reporting of outcomes as numerical representations reduce the complex and dynamic process of educating a child to a mere training exercise. Perhaps it is the difficulty in establishing what constitutes a good education that causes policy-makers and the public alike to be comforted by constricting measures that, ironically, may be compromising the quality of instruction.

This is not intended to diminish the importance of core-skill development. Nonetheless, the current century's demands (e.g., globalism, pluralism, and environmentalism) strongly suggest that policy-makers and educational professionals should return to a more holistic approach to public schooling. Paul Monroe asserts that instructional planning should be tailored to the individual by taking into account:

> ... the development of each member of the coming generation ... [so as to enable him or her] to contribute to developing the highest of all personal possessions, that of a life satisfactory to his [or her] fellows and happy in itself and essential to the perpetuity and progress of society.

As Parker Palmer writes:

> In classical understanding, education [was] the attempt to "lead out" from within the self a core of wisdom that had the power to resist falsehood and live in the light of truth, not by external norms but by reasoned and reflective self-determination.

The essential principle is balance. Current demands upon public-school education require a blending of core-skill development and innovative teaching approaches, grounded in research. Authentic student engagement is achieved by devising structures at the district level that will support ongoing leadership and teachers' professional development. The ultimate goal of every school jurisdiction should be the personalization and optimization of student learning.

Chapter 2

Systemic Thinking:
Essential to Success

"The failure of educational reform derives from a most superficial conception of how complicated settings are organized: their structure, their dynamics, their power relationships, and their underlying values and axioms."

— Seymour B. Sarason

An exceptional organization balances the need for reporting and decision-making structures with a commitment to: 1) directional clarity; 2) continuous learning and innovation; 3) creating a healthy, open atmosphere of emotional safety and trust; 4) delivering superior performance; and 5) effecting significant improvement over time. Such an organization should expand its capacity continually, to attain the desired results. In the words of Peter Senge, Senior Lecturer in Leadership and Sustainability at the MIT Sloan School of Management, it should " … develop new and expanded patterns of thinking … [by which] the collective aspiration is set free, and where people are continually learning how to learn together."

An organization's design should be influenced by research and by best practices. Its goals should be the achievement of long-term results, and of a vibrant work culture that cares deeply about its members. To ensure student success, school districts should develop aligned, collaborative structures that improve schools throughout the system, while preserving their stated objectives.

The primary responsibility of district leadership is to develop and to articulate a vision for the future, as well as to build an organizational architecture capable of responding to new educational challenges. In his book *Inventing Better Schools: An Action Plan for Reform*, Philip C. Schlechty recognizes district leadership's role:

> The way money is allocated, staff members are recruited and assigned, and access to knowledge is distributed cannot be judged in the context of individual schools. Such judgements must be made in the context of the larger systems of which schools are a part, and the solutions to these problems must occur at the systems level as well. Unfortunately, as things now stand, few school districts have the capacities they need to assist at the school level. Unlike schools however, school districts can develop these capacities if district level leaders commit themselves to the task.

The task that Schlechty describes in his book corresponds to that outlined in *Standards For Staff Development: Advancing Student Learning Through Staff Development*, prepared by the National Staff Development Council (now called "Learning Forward"):

> Quality teaching in all classrooms necessitates skillful leadership at the community, district, school, and classroom levels. Ambitious learning goals for students and educators require significant change in curriculum, instruction, assessment, and leadership practices. Leaders at all levels recognize quality professional development as a key strategy for supporting significant improvements. They are able to articulate the critical link between improved student learning and the professional learning of teachers.

Organizational Inquiry Web

To guide the growth of learning organizations, we have designed the *Organizational Inquiry Web*. This Web incorporates the critical elements of systemic thinking: 1) visioning process; 2) shared language construction; 3) organizational design; 4) development of professional capacity; 5) resources acquisition; and 6) monitoring, evaluation, and adaptation. Each element of the Web is interdependent; a change to one can effect change to the others.

The use of this *Organizational Inquiry Web* will result in a vibrant learning organization. Each of the six elements cited above is highlighted and expanded upon separately in the following six chapters. Each chapter presents the relevant research, followed by case examples from our own work experience. The guiding questions provided will stimulate reflection and conversation for your organization's leadership. A corresponding *Organizational Inquiry Rubric* (see page 83-86) supports the *Organizational Inquiry Web's* implementation. Readers are encouraged to review the Rubric as it relates to each chapter. The remaining chapters of this book illustrate and provide context for the key influences and actions that foster organizational coherence.

Organizational Inquiry Web

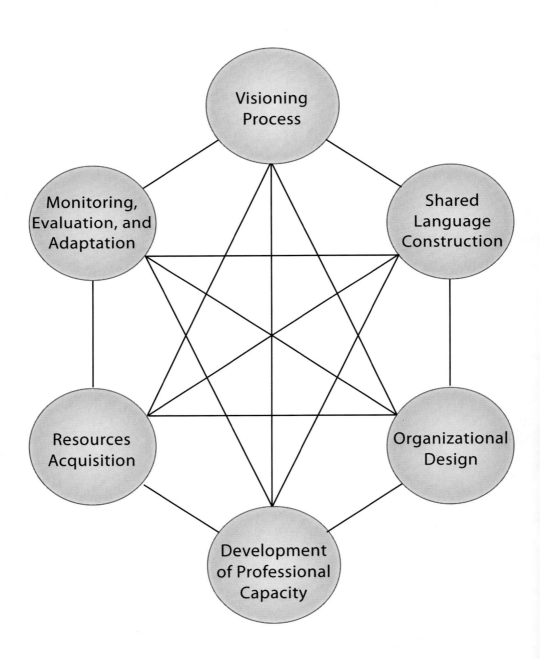

A District's Story

Our work is based upon a school district that has been in operation for over a hundred years. Now one of the largest school districts in Canada, it boasts an enrollment of approximately 70,000 students, from Kindergarten through Grade 12. Located in a large metropolitan area, this district is one of the country's most ethnically, culturally, and economically diverse, and encompasses 125 schools. As over 115 languages are represented, over 15,000 students require English-as-a-Second-Language (ESL) support. Furthermore, there are approximately 7,000 students with Special Needs, and more than 3,000 students are of Aboriginal ancestry.

The school district originally served students throughout a sprawling, rural community. In the 1980s, migration within Canada, as well as immigration — particularly from Asia and South Asia — resulted in substantial population growth. School demographics changed dramatically. At the same time, there was a policy shift in North American public schooling to accommodate students with complex Special Needs. These students had not previously been educated within the regular public-school system.

Like all North American school systems, this district has found itself confronted with changing technologies and with an increasing focus upon academic standards and public accountability. Yet it has striven to fulfill its mandate of preparing students for participation in an ever-changing global community. Predictably, the earlier systemic structures have proven inadequate in the face of the new dynamics.

Saddled with an antiquated operational paradigm, employees struggled to accommodate the profound changes. However, there is a natural resistance to questioning modes of operation that are known to have worked in the past. Moreover, as is widely acknowledged, it is difficult to grasp the scope of change or to understand the implications of a new dynamic until some time has elapsed, affording necessary perspective. To complicate matters still further, the various school-district departments operated predominantly in isolation. There was no unified system. The existing organizational constructs offered limited opportunities for a shared vision or for interdepartmental collaboration toward a common purpose.

In addressing the demands made upon public schooling as a result of the rapid pace of change, the school district has been playing catch-up. Clearly, it now has become necessary to rethink organizational paradigms, but the task of transformative restructuring has proven daunting. In seeking to devise a more aligned and interdependent organizational structure that would accommodate the necessary improvements, we encountered two major hindrances: 1) human and organizational tendencies to preserve the status quo; and 2) limited understanding of how system dynamics and organizational design principles can advance the district's highest priorities.

When departments work together to achieve a common purpose, concerns can readily be identified and improvements made. In January 2009, the above-cited school district conducted a day-long "Service Provider Forum" for personnel from all its educational support departments, in order to examine system alignment and performance. The forum was conducted by an external facilitator with expertise in "Service Provider Interview Matrix" and "Open Space Inquiry."

The participants (comprising approximately seventy-five indivi-duals with various job descriptions) were asked to complete the following sentence so as to generate discussion topics: "*In order to*

effectively work together to build capacity in our schools, I/we need to ... ."
At the end of the session, participants identified the most significant issues that had emerged from their discussions. These were, in descending order of importance:

1. Generating an organizational design (shared plan)
2. Developing teachers' expertise
3. Increasing understanding of student behaviour
4. Defining "quality" schooling
5. Meeting the needs of all students
6. Recognizing and using the staff's expertise
7. Instituting multidisciplinary teams to assist students who are not experiencing success
8. Nurturing the abilities of school leaders
9. Closing the gap between "knowing" and "doing"
10. Fostering student engagement

External Context

Since the 1970s, organizations outside public schooling have been compelled to adapt to similarly unpredictable situations, ushered in by economic and technological advances. Organizational theorists increasingly regard success as being predicated upon the quality of both internal and external networks: in other words, between departments within an organization and across organizations. Schools and school districts are no exception to this principle. In *Change Forces: Probing the Depths of Educational Reform*, author Michael Fullan acknowledges these realities:

> In a rapidly changing society, schools are beginning to discover that new ideas, knowledge creation, and

sharing are essential to solving learning problems. The challenge for educational leaders is how to cultivate and sustain learning under conditions of complex, and rapid change.

Stakeholders in education became intent upon reorganizing schools and school districts in accordance with the new realities. Many observers argued that, to enable teachers to meet the demands of this new society, the education system's basic organizational frameworks would have to be re-invented. School districts found themselves responsible for sponsoring teachers' ongoing professional training.

Unfortunately, it has proven difficult to identify any genuine progress in public-schooling adaptation. William Bennett, former U.S. Secretary of Education, notes that public school systems are notoriously impervious to change:

> The public school establishment is one of the most stubbornly intransigent forces on the planet. It is full of people and organizations dedicated to protecting established programs and keeping things just the way they are. [Educational leaders] talk of reform even as they are circling the wagons to fend off change or preparing to outflank your innovation ...

Even so, a new way of thinking has emerged and has exerted a considerable influence upon public schooling. Peter Senge's book *The Fifth Discipline* won broad-based attention and acceptance. His term "learning organization" provided a much-needed linguistic umbrella for new organizational thinking:

A learning organization is broadly defined by its continuous testing of experience, the transformation of that experience into knowledge that is accessible to the whole organization, and relevant to its core purpose. Learning organizations stress self-reinforcing learning, enabling employees working together in teams to respond to new signals and trends.

The "ideal" learning organization carries profound implications for the redesign of teaching and learning processes, the way school professionals define their roles, and the way schools are structured and regulated.

As is true of many educational-reform movements, the development of learning organizations has, for the most part, not extended beyond the conference room. Educators and administrators still are grappling with this concept and with its implementation. The lack of discernible progress also may be due to the magnitude of the anticipated change.

Where Are We Now?

Over the course of the past few years, we have envisioned and executed a complex restructuring in our areas of responsibility (Student Support Services and aspects of the Curriculum and Instructional Services Centre), which have contributed to the redesign of support structures at the district level. The chief goal of this restructuring has been to offer schools and students more effective support services. Significantly, the improved alignment has engendered a full-service support model for staff and school development and for students in need of strategic interventions.

Ultimately, this restructuring has given our district a more unified and coherent organizational design that will be responsive to future challenges. By following the course of action outlined in this book, the reader will acquire a model strategic plan for an authentic learning organization.

Several reviewers of the *Educere* manuscript have asked how we, as system leaders, were able to implement the process of change, particularly when overcoming resistance or confronting an implementation dip. Our guide for system development has been the *Organizational Inquiry Web* described in this book. The pathway to improvement requires constant vigilance, reflection, and a commitment to action. We have not concerned ourselves unduly with staff resistance or with an implementation dip. Instead, we have devoted our energies to staff collaboration as a means of addressing and working through any opposition to the rhetoric of change. We believe such opposition often is due to a lack of understanding.

Leaders must not be deterred from systemic improvement by such arguments as "Change takes time," or "We have to make sure everyone is ready." Researcher James M. Kaufman has commented upon the human need for prompt, positive reinforcement to motivate actions — otherwise, it's difficult to sustain one's dedication to a shared plan. The hard work of leadership lies in maintaining a commitment to agreed-upon priorities. Too much attention to the change process itself actually may impede progress!

Chapter 3

The Visioning Process:
The Journey Begins

"Vision without action is merely a dream. Action without vision just passes time. Vision with action can change the world."

— Joel Barker

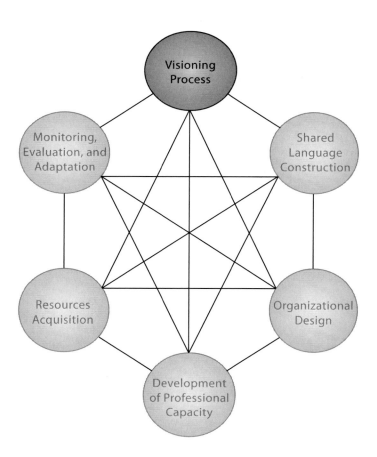

Most organizations recognize the significance of investing time, energy, and careful thought in a collaborative visioning process. This process encompasses mandate clarification (legislative imperative), vision creation (core purpose), articulation of guiding principles (core values), and goal-setting (directional clarity). However, such vital activities are not sufficient. The learning organization must create a comprehensive culture of commitment that commands attention and that compels a translation of ideology into action.

A leader's ability to inspire others is a result of his or her intense focus upon and dedication to the purpose, values, and goals of the desired system. The core purpose must be of enduring value rather than in a continual state of flux. Ultimately, the mandate, vision, guiding beliefs, and goal-setting all are predicated upon the defining question: What is our *raison d'être*? If this answer continually undergoes revision, employees will become frustrated by the leadership's apparent lack of commitment and direction. In their book *Built to Last: Successful Habits of Visionary Companies*, Collins and Porras clearly distinguish "… timeless core values and enduring purpose (which should rarely change) from operating practices and strategies (which should be responsive to a changing world)."

With respect to public schooling, the visioning process must address three essential elements:

Capacity-building is the process by which individuals, groups, organizations, and institutions develop, enhance, and arrange their systems, resources, and knowledge. It reflects their abilities, individually and collectively, to perform functions, to solve problems, and to achieve objectives.

Organizations that have attended to the demands of these interrelated elements of the visioning process can assess whether individual or communal actions continue to meet the stated goals. (For a discussion of the assessment of organizational outcomes, please see Chapter 8 – Monitoring, Evaluation, and Adaptation: Determining Quality.)

Visioning Elements

Mandate Clarification
As part of the visioning process, the public sector should ensure that legislative or policy requirements are reviewed by the leadership.

Examples:

Statement of Education Policy Order
The purpose of the British Columbia school system is to enable learners to develop their individual potential and to acquire the knowledge, skills, and attitudes needed to contribute to a healthy society and a prosperous and sustainable economy.

School Act (Special Needs Student Order MI150/89)
2. (2) A board must provide a student with special needs with an educational program in a classroom where that student is integrated with other students who do not have special needs.

B.C. Ministry of Education Special Education Policy
All students should have equitable access to learning, opportunities for achievement, and the pursuit of educational excellence in all aspects of their educational program.

Vision Creation

Vision creation entails a reflective, collaborative process that results in a succinct articulation of the organization's *raison d'être* and its desired goals. Its vision will determine the organization's future direction.

Example:

The school district is dedicated to the promotion of inclusive, equitable, and effective education for all students. As one aspect of its holistic approach, our Board and senior staff have envisioned a Student Support Services department that, while conforming to the Ministry's determination of appropriate services, is responsive to the students' individual needs.

Student Support Services personnel are committed to working collaboratively with families, community agencies, and school staff to assist students with diverse needs in reaching their academic and social potentials. The unique insights and perspectives provided by parents enable them to act not only as advocates for their children, but as invaluable partners in this evolving and responsive process.

Guiding Beliefs

Guiding beliefs, which define core values, align with, and expand upon the organization's vision.

Examples:

- As a fundamental principle, public schooling must embrace diversity in all its forms.
- Public schooling must be structured in ways that are aligned, coherent, and sustainable.
- Capacity-building is critical in order to support diversity in public schooling.
- School-district actions must promote the primacy of the classroom environment, maintaining a clear focus upon student learning.
- Resources are allocated most effectively when determined according to system analysis, incorporating equity parameters (i.e., school demographics, diverse needs, language, and economic differences).
- With diversity as the norm, a rigid delineation of staff roles and responsibilities is not feasible. Instead, staff members should share their duties and expertise, to assist students with diverse needs.

Goal-setting

Goal-setting provides directional clarity and promotes a results-based framework for assessment. Attainable goals will serve to motivate personnel throughout the organization.

Examples:

- Restructure district departments so as to facilitate the use of the *District/School Development Framework.*
- Design and implement a district-wide strategy to enhance professional learning, with a focus upon learning assessment and differentiation of instruction.

- Develop and implement district standards and best-practice rubrics for program development for Learner Support Team, School-Based Team, and Counselling Services.

Our Development Journey

An adage of Henry David Thoreau's illustrates the importance of setting direction: " … [Y]ou only hit what you aim at." In other words: If you don't know where you are going, you surely will not get there.

Faced with the noted complexities that confront our school district, we found ourselves asking: What is the role of public schooling? Clearly, public schooling is not the sole answer to all of the community's economic, social, and other challenges. Nonetheless, an excellent public school system will contribute immeasurably toward enabling our students to meet society's future needs.

Therefore, our journey began with a proposal for structural realignment that would result in the merger of disparate district departments. We also initiated a process of reviewing the mandate for public schooling. Surprisingly, there had not been a systematic review of the legislative mandate with regard to the interrelationship of other core components of the visioning process. Instead, each element of the process appeared isolated. Such a lack of systemic and coherent planning precluded the attainment of specific goals.

We have found that ongoing conversation with personnel, whether individuals, small groups, or an entire staff, has served to hone our shared vision and guiding beliefs, and has generated enhanced goal-setting and interdepartmental collaboration.

While much has been written regarding the shared development of vision and goal-setting, the important task of articulating guiding beliefs often is overlooked. Yet we have discovered this aspect to be crucial in translating the philosophical underpinnings of vision to more tangible value statements, thus enabling us to evaluate actions and to progress toward our stated goals.

The visioning process — inclusive of mandate clarification, vision creation, guiding beliefs development, and goal-setting — has become the implied contract defining our collective responsibilities. It replaces individual agendas and disparate departmental actions with a far broader commitment to school improvement, to staff development, and to student success.

Guiding Questions

These questions are intended to stimulate reflection when applying the concepts outlined in each chapter. They also may be used to foster conversations within an organization, thus assisting both its leadership and the individual reader in examining existing structures and practices, and in identifying what remains to be accomplished.

- What district processes have been established to define mandate, vision, guiding beliefs, and goals?

- What district processes are being implemented to test and to refine shared beliefs on an ongoing basis?

- How do mandate, vision, and guiding beliefs influence goal-setting (district priorities)?

Chapter 4

Shared Language Construction:
From Vision to Action

*" ... A fundamental task of the organization is [to deal efficiently]
with information and decisions ... "*

— Ikujiro Nonaka

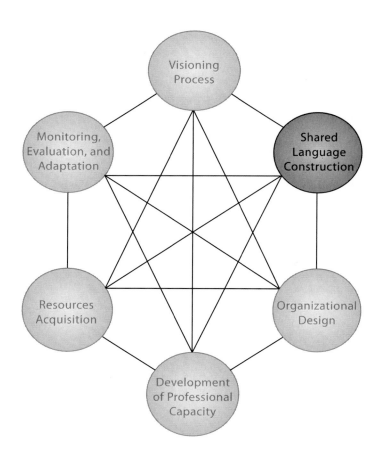

In order to move from vision to action, an organization must devise a shared language. Leadership should guide the collaborative development of two equally important facets: 1) the crafting of organizational maxims that encompass the enterprise's fundamental beliefs; and 2) the development of codified, procedural language (explicit knowledge) that converts mandate, policy, and guidelines into practice. The resultant shared language will facilitate organizational clarity and effectiveness. Ikujiro Nonaka contends:

> ... Organizational creation of knowledge ... should be focused on the active, subjective nature of knowledge represented by such terms as "belief" and "commitment" that are deeply rooted in the value systems of individuals.

Only when this clarity is established will team members with divergent skill sets and expertise (substantive knowledge) be able to navigate the collaborative process confidently.

Organizational Maxims

Organizational maxims that possess an enduring and inspirational quality will advance the group narrative. When used strategically, such axioms impart an underlying set of core values, and affect employees' actions accordingly. They also promote a sense of identification with a values-rich culture, allowing its members to cite "the way we do things around here."

Our Favourite Organizational Maxims:

- "For children, schooling is not only preparation for life — it *is* life."

- "When dealing with difficult people, let empathy with appropriate boundaries guide your interactions."

- "Avoid doing for children what they can do for themselves, it can be disrespectful."

- "Crisis often generates opportunity."

- "Without understanding, there can be no vision."

Procedural Documents

Procedural documents expand upon the organizational maxims by clarifying the mandate, policy, procedures, and guidelines. These documents state and implement operational goals and imperatives. They delineate roles and responsibilities system-wide, enabling a collaborative process.

Examples:

- Detailing procedures for policy development or revision
- Defining expectations for productive consultation and collaboration with parents
- Describing respectful discipline and suspension processes that employ the elements of procedural fairness
- Developing best-practice service manuals and rubrics in specialized areas
- Outlining school-district appeal procedures, as required by legislation

Example (Sample Document):

Consultation/Collaboration

"Consultation is a process, not an event."

Recent court cases have defined the extent of a school district's responsibility to consult and to collaborate with parents of a student with Special Needs. Consultation and collaboration must be commensurate with a student's level of disability, as well as with the degree of individualization that his or her education plan requires (i.e., ranging from mild adaptations to a significantly modified educational program).

Principles:

- Parents must be consulted before any decision is made regarding their child's placement within the school system, and before preparation of the Individualized Education Plan (IEP).

- In a productive consultation, each side must attempt to demonstrate that its proposal effectively supports the student's learning. When thoughtful collaboration takes place with a view to what is in the student's best interest, clarity often emerges naturally.

- If agreement is not reached during consultation with the parents, the school district maintains the right to determine a student's placement. The parents of a child with Special Needs do not have the right of veto over placement or IEP decisions.

- In the absence of complete agreement, the school district must continue to work toward a win-win solution.

- Parents and the school district have a mutual obligation to provide timely information and to make whatever accommodations are necessary to establish an educational program that is in the best interests of the child.

Decisions regarding educational programming and/or IEP development require the collective wisdom of educational professionals in consultation with families.

Our Development Journey

We chronicled which axioms best expressed our guiding beliefs, and incorporated them into our interactions with the staff. We also designed procedural documents such as memos, best-practice rubrics, department policy manuals, newsletters, procedural handbooks, and inter-agency protocols. These communications often were generated by collaborative development processes, which, like the maxims, fostered shared understanding

To communicate the newly-consolidated organizational or departmental identity, corporate branding elements such as logo, colours, motto, and letterhead have proven very useful. Branding is a bridge between the visioning process and procedural language, and it imparts a professional image. Additionally, we established an online resource for administrators, teachers, parents, and students. This electronic repository allows for ease of access to, and broad-based dissemination of, important organizational documents.

Once "the way we do things around here" was explained in writing, our staff and personnel throughout the district were able to perform with greater confidence and to devote more time to effective, collaborative practices. The influential power of shared language allows for a deep appreciation of the visioning process and for a natural progression from vision to action.

Guiding Questions

- What organizational maxims are being used, or might be considered, to communicate organizational principles?

- What subjects should the procedural documents address?

- Are procedural documents being distributed as efficiently as possible?

Chapter 5

Organizational Design:
Form Follows Function

"The responsibility for improving systems resides solely with leadership. 85% of the problems you encounter in your organization are system problems, not caused by human inadequacies."

— W. Edwards Deming

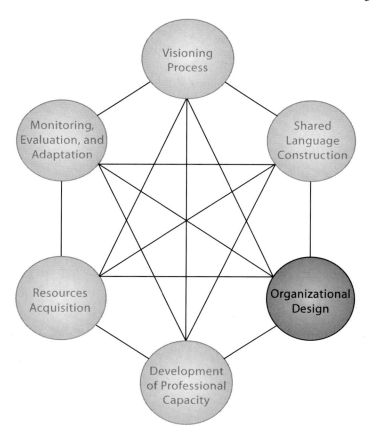

A successful organizational design integrates structural and conceptual elements that result from mandate, vision, guiding beliefs, and goal-setting. The design or architecture (form) should further the declared purposes (function) and should be constructed so as to promote: 1) multidisciplinary teaming; 2) flexible boundaries and role release (i.e., assigning specific tasks and methods usually performed by one person on a child's team to other team members); 3) a professional culture committed to a balance between relationships and results; 4) the exchange or transfer of innovative ideas; and 5) continuous learning.

School districts are responsible for configuring themselves in ways that advance research-based, professional learning and that facilitate student development, engagement, and education. Collaborative teams should consist of well-qualified, responsive personnel and should offer a continuum of professional-development activities aligned with the district's highest priorities. Local context is a significant factor in these organizational designs. Larger school districts clearly have the advantage of possessing a larger number of practitioners with diverse kinds of expertise that can be shared.

Influences upon School Learning

Using evidence accumulated from sixty-one research experts, as well as from ninety-one meta-analyses and from 179 chapter reviews — detailing a total of 11,000 relationships — Wang, Haertel, and Walberg identified the ten educational, psychological, and social factors that most profoundly affect student learning:

1. Classroom management
2. Meta-cognitive processes
3. Cognitive processes

4. Home/parental support
5. Student/teacher social interaction
6. Social/behavioural attributes
7. Motivation
8. Peer group
9. Instruction methods and quality
10. School culture

To engage students in activities that broaden knowledge and that hone critical skills, successful teaching must integrate various curriculum designs, instructional methodologies, assessment practices, and classroom-management strategies.

Conceptual Framework for District and School Development

School principals, staff, and parent representatives are responsible for the collaborative development of a school plan. Yet district leadership, too, must share in this responsibility, since any true improvement can be achieved only in alignment with the school district's goals and best practices. The district's human and monetary resources should be allocated accordingly. The school district's definitions of "quality" and "the need for improvement" then become critical. What actions are being taken, or are being planned, to identify these needs and to realize these ends?

To define successful schooling, we have designed an innovative *District/School Development Framework* that combines a cornerstone of current educational thought, namely the *Universal Design for Learning*, with our own original ideas, which have termed Components of Quality Schools. The synthesis of these two constructs provides a conceptual mapping for a framework that promotes symbiotic district and school development.

Universal Design for Learning (UDL)

The *Universal Design for Learning* is a practical, research-based framework for responding to individual learning differences. It promotes the analysis and development of a wide range of services: from Universal, through Targeted, to Intensive.

Universal practices and supports address the majority of system- and school-based development issues (e.g., curriculum, instruction, assessment, and behavioural support). A commitment to Universal teaching practices is fundamental to quality public schooling.

Targeted practices and supports are focused, individual, or group strategies that are based upon, and that contribute to, Universal actions. The intent of Targeted supports is to align with, and to compound the effects of, Universal practices, such as reading and writing interventions.

Intensive practices and supports are based upon, and contribute to, Universal and Targeted supports. Typically, these practices are highly individualized and specialized (i.e., student- or context-specific). These Intensive supports also are designed to align with, and to compound the effects of, Universal and Targeted practices.

UDL Support Continuum

Intensive
practices/supports
5% +/-

Targeted
practices/supports
15% +/-

Universal
practices/supports
80% +/-

Components of Quality Schools (CQS)

The Components of Quality Schools consist of research-supported areas of focus that are vital to public schooling. These components may be analyzed either separately or through an integrated approach. Included after the description of each component is a title for recommended further reading.

"Curriculum" is a pathway that leads to the attainment of core domains of knowledge integral to our democratic society. It defines what students are expected to know, to understand, and to do during a particular course of study.

> Recommended reading:
> *Understanding by Design: Professional Development Workbook*
> by Jay McTighe and Grant Wiggins

"Instruction" requires proactively planning and executing varied approaches to content, process, and product in anticipation of student differences in readiness, interest, and learning needs.

> Recommended reading:
> *Integrating Differentiating Instruction + Understanding by Design: Connecting Content and Kids*
> by Carol Ann Tomlinson and Jay McTighe

"Assessment" is the systematic process of gathering information in order to make appropriate educational decisions regarding student learning. Assessment is comprehensive, ranging from informal to standardized formal assessments, which lead to evaluation (e.g., teacher appraisal of student progress).

Recommended reading:
Classroom Assessment for Student Learning: Doing It Right – Using It Well
by Richard Stiggins, Judith Arter, Jan Chappuis, and Stephen Chappuis

"Emotional and Social Development" promotes healthy growth and interaction for all students, both in the classroom and throughout the school and the district. It teaches honesty, integrity, tolerance, appreciation of individual differences, caring about others, and acceptance of responsibility.

Recommended reading:
Social Intelligence: The New Science of Human Relationships
by Daniel Goldman

"Aboriginal Support" requires that all stakeholders commit themselves to advancing a shared vision that reflects cultural sensitivities and that encompasses the belief that all Aboriginal students can achieve success.

Recommended reading:
Aboriginal Education: Fulfilling the Promise
by Marlene Brant Castellano, Lynne Davis, and Louise Lahache

"Technology" plays various significant roles in public-schooling processes (e.g., access, supporting engagement and learning, innovation, and effective communication).

Recommended reading:
Empowering Students with Technology
by Alan C. November

"**Specialized Support**" pertains to knowledge, skills, or services that provide a specific type of support (e.g., orientation and mobility, augmentative communication, adaptive technology).

> Recommended reading:
> *Best Practices in School Psychology V*
> by Alex Thomas and Jeff Grimes

"**Parents and Community**," as partners in education, assist in student learning, improve school programs, and forge connections between the school and the larger community.

> Recommended reading:
> *School, Family, and Community Partnerships: Preparing Educators and Improving Schools*
> by Joyce Epstein

"**Other**" is a catch-all category that reflects the school community and its contextual needs.

> Recommended reading:
> *Critical Thinking: How to Prepare for a Rapidly Changing World*
> by Richard W. Paul

District/School Development Framework

Individually, UDL and CQS hold significant promise as planning tools for educators. However, their effectiveness is more fully realized when they are integrated into the *District/School Development Framework*. The combination of these constructs enables a conceptual mapping that provides the clarity essential to capacity-building and to system development.

The *District/School Development Framework* provides a visual mapping of core areas for focus. This framework may be scaled as needed, and is valuable in guiding planning and development at various system levels:

- District-wide
- District department
- School-wide
- School department
- Classroom

A system-wide or site-based analysis of the Components of Quality Schools, when viewed through the *Universal Design for Learning* continuum, will assist in the crafting of a realistic development plan. Professional-development activities can be plotted on the framework by:

1. selecting an area for focus from the Components of Quality Schools; and
2. selecting activities from the *Universal Design for Learning* support continuum.

Example:

Supporting diverse learner needs, with a focus upon reading instruction:

1. Components of Quality Schools (Area for Focus): **Instruction**
2. *Universal Design for Learning* (Activities):

Universal	▶	Differentiated Instruction (Reading Focus)
Targeted	▶	Focused Interventions to Support Reading
Intensive	▶	Adaptive Technology to Support Reading

District/School Development Framework

	Curriculum	Instruction	Assessment	Emotional/ Social Development
U N I V E R S A L		Differentiated Instruction		
T A R G E T E D		Focused Reading Interventions		
I N T E N S I V E		Adaptive Technology to Support Reading		

Aboriginal Support	Technology	Specialized Support	Parenting/Community	Other

Our Development Journey

The structural and conceptual components of organizational design are equally important. The following account is an example of the fragmentation of departmental responsibilities.

The Special Education portfolio (administering programs and services for students with Special Needs) historically had been the responsibility of three district departments: Special Education, Student Services, and the Curriculum and Instructional Services Centre. Each of these departments maintained separate referral and designation processes, and rarely collaborated. Their progress toward structural alignment is detailed below.

Journey to Alignment (Structural):

Special Education Supports and Services

Prior to 2003

Special Education – SPED
- Autism Spectrum Disorder
- Deaf or Hard of Hearing
- Deafblind
- Mild Intellectual Disabilities
- Moderate to Profound Intellectual Disabilities
- Physical Disabilities/Chronic Health Impairments
- Physically Dependent – Multiple Needs
- Visual Impairments

A

B

Student Services – SS
- Intensive Behaviour/Serious Mental Illness
- Moderate Behaviour/Mental Illness

C

Curriculum & Instructional Services Centre – CISC
- Gifted
- Learning Disabilities

2003 to 2006

A+B

Student Support Services – SSS (merger of SPED and SS)
- Autism Spectrum Disorder
- Deaf or Hard of Hearing
- Deafblind
- Intensive Behaviour/Serious Mental Illness
- Mild Intellectual Disabilities
- Moderate Behaviour/Mental Illness
- Moderate to Profound Intellectual Disabilities
- Physical Disabilities/Chronic Health Impairments
- Physically Dependent – Multiple Needs
- Visual Impairments

C

Curriculum & Instructional Services Centre – CISC
- Gifted
- Learning Disabilities

2007 to Present

Student Support Services (combination of SSS and the elements of CISC responsible for diversity)

A+B+C

- Autism Spectrum Disorder
- Deaf or Hard of Hearing
- Deafblind
- Gifted
- Intensive Behaviour/Serious Mental Illness
- Learning Disabilities
- Mild Intellectual Disabilities
- Moderate Behaviour/Mental Illness
- Moderate to Profound Intellectual Disabilities
- Physical Disabilities/Chronic Health Impairments
- Physically Dependent – Multiple Needs
- Visual Impairments

Integration of Special Education Programs and Services

The confluence of *visioning + shared language + organizational design* is illustrated by the following scenario: We envisioned the re-organization of a number of district departments. With all Special Education programs and services now our supervisory responsibility, we determined that we could simplify access to services, system-wide, by reducing the number of referral forms required to access various services. School personnel had been struggling with the frustration of having to complete one of the eight forms listed below:

- School Psychology Services
- Speech-Language Pathology Services
- Behaviour Supports/Designations
- Gifted Programs/Services
- Occupational/Physical Therapy Services
- Special Education Designation or Special Programs
- Student Services Special Programs
- Pre-school Transitions

These referral forms that we "inherited" had, for the most part, been developed by teachers or staff members with limited administrative oversight, no internal or external assessment of needs, no procedural standardization, no common terminology, and no corporate branding. Each of the forms existed in numerous iterations, having evolved over time. One of the documents was developed with the expressed goal of "being so difficult to complete as to reduce the number of referrals received." School personnel responsible for completion of these applications felt hindered in their attempts to access services and support for students in need.

How Did We Achieve a Solution?

We met with the various departments to determine their needs and to address expressed concerns about "giving up" their tailored referral forms. We also established a focus group, inviting a sample of school personnel to provide input. By means of listening, reassurance, collaboration, conducting an external review of referral forms, drafting, and field testing, we succeeded in designing a common referral form that met all requisite field and departmental needs.

What Results Were Yielded by This Accomplishment?

- System-wide efficiency and streamlined access to services for students requiring support
- Confidence in the system (including reduction of frustration)
- Clarity regarding the distinction between administrative responsibilities and the work of employees
- Departmental professionalization (e.g., usability, branding, online repository)
- Commitment to shared or aligned practices, with a focus upon system-wide collaboration and system responsiveness

The Next Crucial Steps

Subsequent to structural realignment, we began the visioning process and the development of shared language. Next, we identified the public-schooling organization's attainable goals, of which "student learning" clearly was the most important. Yet there is much research indicating that the improvement of universal classroom teaching practice is equally essential.

We developed an action plan accordingly. A literature review dedicated to identifying the current best thinking on organizing for success precipitated discussion with our staff regarding a multidisciplinary approach. This resulted in the sharing of expertise, whose purpose was to provide improved support to schools and to students in need.

The next developmental step required that teams of professionals operate throughout the district, aligned with our conceptual framework, to assist with school and staff development. When we did not possess internal capacity in a particular area of critical focus (e.g., differentiation of instruction), resources were allocated to allow the staff to acquire the necessary expertise.

Journey to Alignment (Conceptual):

Much of this work was new to us and to our school district. Given the rapid changes to which British Columbia's public schooling was compelled to respond, initiatives often were prompted from outside the school district rather than by an internal review of teacher development or of school practices.

We examined the research to establish which district-level actions would have the greatest impact upon student learning. We chose the conceptual framework of the *Universal Design for Learning* (UDL), with the integration of the Components of Quality Schools (CQS). These ideas have been favourably received by the education department at a major university, classroom teachers, school principals, district leadership, a provincial Special Education leadership organization, and a national educational consortium. Each group confirmed the viability of our *District/School Development Framework*. Serving as a legitimate test of validity, this informed, objective consensus is most encouraging.

Staff members then were asked to plot all professional-development activities for which they were responsible, in alignment with the *District/School Development Framework*. Although our support teachers voiced the need for system development and for capacity-building at the Universal level, many proved to be operating primarily as responders rather than as initiators and were hesitant to embrace a multidisciplinary role. The synthesis of UDL and CQS served as a catalyst for the re-envisioning of their roles, transforming them from responders at the Targeted and Intensive levels to capacity-builders across the entire UDL spectrum.

Multidisciplinary teams now are meeting with assistant super-intendents in order to foster school development. The intended future direction is a restructuring of all district-level educational services, to ensure that they are connected to school planning and development.

Guiding Questions

- What are research-supported practices at the Universal, Targeted, and Intensive levels for each of the components of quality schools?

- What organizational strategy has been implemented to support school development?

- How do the conceptual and structural designs of your organization support quality schooling?

Chapter 6

Development of Professional Capacity: Fostering Student Engagement

"Teachers cannot create and sustain the conditions for productive development of children if those conditions do not exist for teachers."

— Seymour B. Sarason

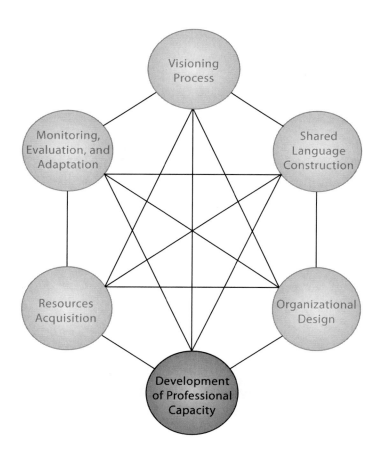

University or college preparation and training programs are intended to provide a base of core knowledge, skills, and competencies required by a particular field of study. While critically important, these skills and competencies often prove to be insufficient relative to the real-world demands of the relevant profession.

Since quality organizations are, by definition, learning organizations, the fundamental duty of such entities must be the continuous development of their employees' knowledge and skills. This is especially true of public schools. In their book *District Leadership That Works: Striking the Right Balance*, Marzano and Walters reinforce this view:

> Districts must ensure that the necessary resources, including time, money, personnel, and materials are allocated to accomplish the district's goals. It is clear ... that a meaningful commitment of funding must be dedicated to professional development for teachers and principals. Professional development should focus on building the requisite knowledge, skills, and competencies teachers and principals need to accomplish the district goals. Furthermore, professional development resources deployed at the school level must be used in ways that *align with district goals.*

The teachers' duties include: mastery of the pillars of pedagogy (curriculum, instruction, assessment, and classroom management); demonstration of high ethical standards; and a commitment to ongoing, collaborative learning and to skills development. It should be noted that the employees' autonomy must be balanced with their responsibilities to the organization. (For further discussion, please see Chapter 10 – The Professional Teacher: Rights and Responsibilities.)

The Learning Process

Detailed phenomenological studies indicate that the human learning process consists of five levels. According to Dreyfus and Dreyfus, each of these levels is characterized by recognizable behaviours and degrees of ability:

1. **Novice**
    - rigidly adheres to rules
    - has limited discretional judgement

2. **Advanced Beginner**
    - still demonstrates limited situational perception
    - addresses task components separately and assigns them equal importance

3. **Competent Performer**
    - responds adequately to information or work overload
    - partially understands action as part of longer-term goals
    - executes conscious, deliberate planning

4. **Proficient Performer**
    - views situation holistically, rather than focusing upon its disparate elements
    - perceives the essence of an issue or situation
    - is guided by organizational maxims

5. **Expert**
    - no longer is reliant upon rules, guidelines, or maxims
    - possesses an intuitive grasp of situation
    - envisions possibilities

This progression represents a gradual transition from rigid adherence to rules to a mode of intuitive reasoning. Some people do not attain the highest level of proficiency in their chosen fields.

Effective Practices for Transmission of Teachers' Knowledge and Skills

Professional-development activities should be based upon current research findings. As approximately 60% of teachers' knowledge has been found to be of a tacit (implied) nature, it most effectively is transmitted interpersonally when embedded in authentic experiences, in an environment of trust. While tacit knowledge incorporates both cognitive and technical elements, explicit knowledge is codified, and thus requires a more direct communication of information. These observations significantly affect a school district's approach toward professional development. The transfer of teachers' knowledge and skills into practice should occur within a framework that includes a balance of activities, building from awareness through to peer mentoring.

How knowledge and skills are transferred to teachers:

- Awareness/Information transfer – 10% (explicit)
- Demonstration/Model – 10%
- Practice/Feedback – 20%
- Peer mentoring in the classroom – 60% (tacit)

Two Aspects of Knowledge Transfer

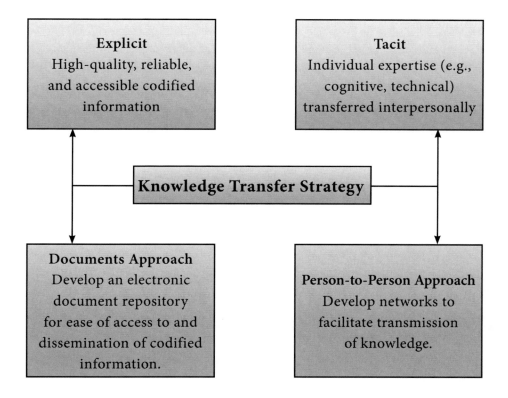

Professional Development Continuum

Today's classroom environment reflects an ever-adapting society charged to respond to, among other factors, English-language learners, Special Education, and Diverse Learners, and an explosion in knowledge and in technology. In order to teach effectively in such an environment, teachers must be equipped with the knowledge and skills necessary to engage all students in the learning process. Although teacher-education programs provide educators with a base set of knowledge and skills, scholarly teaching develops over time and requires attention to theory, research, instructional design, learning styles, methods of assessment, child development, and classroom management. Consequently, school districts are urged to design and to implement a research-based, incremental framework that will provide focus and clarity in the areas of: 1) teacher development; and 2) student development, engagement, and learning.

As educational professionals and system leaders, we have created the *Professional Development Continuum*, which includes: 1) expert speakers; 2) conference teaming; 3) content-focused in-service; 4) networks of practice; 5) collaborative professional learning; and 6) peer mentoring. This Continuum progresses from ideas and inspiration to authentic change and enduring impact. Critical to the Continuum's success is the district's significant investment of resources in the professional-development activities that align with research-based teaching practices.

Professional Development Continuum

Enduring Impact

Greater
Focus

Tacit

Resourcing Professional Development (time and money)

Positive Transfer of Knowledge to Practice

Peer Mentoring
- Tacit, positive transfer
- Practitioner-to-practitioner

Collaborative Professional Learning
- Guided inquiry (outcome-based)
- Site-specific

Networks of Practice
- Facilitated specificity
- Professional talk

Content-focused In-service
- Procedural/substantive focus
- Explicit-knowledge transfer

Conference Teaming
- Reinforces concept of learning organization
- Aggregates momentum

Expert Speakers
- Inspiration/motivation
- Directional momentum

Lesser
Focus

Awareness

Explicit

Key Aspects of the Professional Development Continuum

Expert Speakers:
Presentations by expert speakers — international, national, and local — will generate wide interest and motivation in cultivating new learning habits and teaching practices.

Conference Teaming:
Conference teaming strategically seeds fertile ground. Sending a team of district leaders and teachers to important conferences significantly increases momentum toward a desired goal.

Content-focused In-service:
Content-focused in-service enhances teachers' instruction strategies, in addition to their knowledge of pedagogical content.

Networks of Practice:
Networks of practice (district focus) are professional networks whose members interact by sharing information that assists them in the performance of their work. These complex, interrelated structures encompass: 1) a topical focus; 2) emotionally safe relationships; 3) a commitment to open collaboration; 4) a format of inquiry; 5) leadership; and 6) a focus upon professional learning.

Collaborative Professional Learning:
Collaborative professional learning (site-specific) seeks to increase teacher motivation, success, efficacy and satisfaction, both by developing a shared school vision and by building a team actively engaged in pursuit of the stated goals. The professional learning community must dedicate itself to forging an innovative, collaborative, and interdependent culture.

Peer Mentoring:

Peer mentoring (i.e., teachers learning from one another) is achieved by means of: 1) a theoretical basis for new skill or strategy; 2) the modeling or demonstration of new skills; 3) practice simulation; 4) structured review and constructive feedback; and 5) hands-on, in-class assistance with the implementation of newly acquired skills.

While job-imbedded peer mentoring is the most effective method of imparting one teacher's knowledge and skills to another, it is also the most difficult practice to implement systematically. Yet, because it is paramount, the transmission of knowledge must prevail over considerations of logistics, cost, and any staff resistance or collective agreements.

Acknowledging the value of teacher development and peer mentoring, Learning Forward (formerly The National Staff Development Council) advocates that districts dedicate at least 10% of their budgets to staff development. This reflects our own belief that the importance of creating structures to support teacher development cannot be overstated. One of the main purposes of this book is to encourage district-level leaders to embrace the notion that teacher development is the critical factor in enhanced outcomes for students. Marzano and Waters concur in this view, stating:

> ... The only way to improve outcomes is to improve instruction ... Interventions are effective in achieving this ... [By] coaching classroom practice, moving teacher training to the classroom, developing stronger school leaders, and enabling teachers to learn from each other, [effective systems] have found ways to deliver these interventions ...

A number of innovative strategies may be designed and implemented on scales determined by such local factors as the district's size, access to university partnerships, teacher collective agreements, and union relationships. Such innovations may include:

- Job-embedded peer mentoring for novice teachers. The site-specific, expert teachers (or those from elsewhere in the school district) enlisted to act as peer mentors in the classroom will require release time.

- District-designed professional-development modules (simulations) for peer mentoring. These would specifically address the integration of curriculum design, assessment and evaluation of student performance, differentiation of instruction necessitated by diverse needs, and differentiation of classroom-management strategies.

- A district/university partnership (Teaching Institute) that entails an additional year of teacher training for novice teachers hired by the district. Potential compensation for additional training would be dictated by collective agreements.

Learner Support Teams

The confluence of the *visioning process + shared language + organizational design + development of professional capacity* is illustrated by the following account: During the 2001-2002 school year, a newly elected provincial government enacted public-schooling legislation that, in our district, had the effect of decreasing by a quarter the English-as-a-Second-Language, Learning Assistance, and Learning Disabilities staffing. At the same time, our district had transformed its model for services offered to students in need of academic support. The district envisioned a research-based, full-service model in which professionals collaborated and expertise was shared, thus providing students with significantly enhanced instructional support. All ESL teachers, teachers supporting students with Learning Disabilities, and teachers of students requiring Learning Assistance now were designated as "Learning Support Teachers." The 300 such professionals remaining in our school district regarded the new conceptual model primarily as a means to cut staffing levels. Yet the number of students requiring focused instructional support, in particular ESL instruction, had increased exponentially.

Each of the following four years (2003 through 2006) witnessed a change in school-district Directors of Instruction, and each subsequent Director determined his or her own LST staffing-allocation procedures. The turnover in leadership, and the reduced number of Learning Support Teachers occasioned by the budget cuts, rendered virtually impossible the development of any coherent leadership vision with regard to learning-support services.

In 2006, in order to establish a much-needed continuum of academic support, we adopted the research-based *Universal Design for Learning* framework. Our intent was to define the Learning Support Teachers' roles and functions, and to align student-support structures so as to effect quality academic interventions. Our primary objectives were the *prevention* of learning challenges, the *remediation* of existing learning difficulties, curriculum *adaptation* to accommodate students by means of more intensive learning supports, and focused ESL instruction. We recognized the need for a more holistic and collaborative approach that would enable schools to coordinate the Learning Support Teachers' roles with other specialized support services, such as those offered by the Speech-Language Pathologists, School Psychologists, and Special Education Integration Support Teachers and Counsellors.

Since professionals in various specialized roles have differing approaches, and perhaps even divergent views, as to how best to support students with learning challenges, we sought to develop a common understanding: expressed, for instance, by shared language. Aided by staff input, we created a Handbook of Guidelines and Procedures for Learning Support Team Teachers, to clarify the parameters of their responsibilities and to foster pedagogical improvements. Additionally, we implemented procedural processes by introducing "talking sticks." These one- or two-page communication tools addressed such issues as the role and functions of a Case Manager, and procedures for consultation and collaboration between parents and the school district regarding students with Special Needs. We also developed "best practices" Rubrics concerning Learner Support Teams, School-Based Teams, and counselling services; research-based newsletters; and an online repository to facilitate district-wide access to these resources.

We succeeded in expanding the staffing complement of Learning Support Helping Teachers (i.e., district-based consultants), attracting personnel whose expertise advanced our strategic plan. Upon discovering that their specialized skills were not offered across the spectrum of Kindergarten through Grade 12, we applied a Zonal Model that was included in our structural Organizational Design, to advance district-wide access to these services. The Zonal Model was designed to allow district-based experts to share practices in the best interest of students who required instructional support, thus enhancing the capacity of LST teachers across the system.

We generated a thematic professional-development structure at district, school, and individual levels. This was the genesis of the *District/School Development Framework*. Then, consulting with school principals, we determined how staffing should be allocated so as to accord with each school's equity parameters (i.e., student composites that constitute vulnerability indexes). The new model replaced the practice of *ad hoc* staffing allocations based upon "impressions of need." The resourcing transparency that resulted from this equitable, systematic process and from our data analysis instilled new confidence. Additionally, occasional "mock" audits were conducted, to establish whether statutory obligations regarding educational planning were, in fact, being met at the school level.

The "Best Practices" development Rubrics and the Learning Support Teachers' Handbook of Guidelines and Procedures enabled the district's consultant teachers to become engaged in conversations about "best practices" at the district and school levels. This involvement led to greater efficacy and improved results of the teaching teams' work as a whole, facilitating the monitoring, evaluation, and adaptation of school services to better meet students' needs.

Our Development Journey

The creation of coherent structural and conceptual designs, and a vision of school, leadership, and teacher development, are fundamental to the establishment of a productive learning organization. Archaic practices must be replaced by the understanding that capacity-building is both a shared commitment and a continually evolving process. It demands a collaborative infrastructure at the district level, and a multidisciplinary approach at the school level.

In bringing specialized staff together and in instituting a conceptual framework to structure our collective thinking, we now can accurately assess the status of development activities system-wide. Before the introduction of this system-alignment process, the lack of focused planning for school and teacher development also resulted in a significant overlap and duplication of activities. The new structural and conceptual alignment yields the following outcomes: 1) system efficiency; 2) focused professional-development opportunities to improve teaching practices; 3) teacher collaboration and the sharing of expertise; and 4) increased communication, transparency, and efficacy in the shared work of school development.

The next step in our development process was the establishment of trust among the members of our multidisciplinary teams. They have also been encouraged to envision new professional practices. Over time, staff conversations have progressed from topics such as the viability and purpose of working together to more reflective, professional discussions of how best to nurture teachers and schools at various stages of development. Collaboration, timing, patience, and clarity of the strategic plan all have been essential in overcoming a natural resistance to change.

The traditional professional-development paradigm no longer appeared adequate. Commonly referred to as the "Train and Hope" methodology, this approach consisted of sending educators to lectures and seminars that introduced promising practices. It was hoped that such "training" would lead to improved classroom outcomes. Yet our review of research regarding the learning process suggested otherwise. Consequently, we designed the *Professional Development Continuum*. Since district resources are used best when devoted to teacher mentoring and to networks, plans for systemic development should offer additional training to novices and expert practitioners alike.

This new model of mentorship and of network support represents a departure from the devoid-of-context "Tell me" standard in favour of a real-time "Show me" practice.

However, recognizing that all implementation plans are processes with many phases, and that a commitment to system-wide staff development requires vigilance over time, significant commitment will be required at the district level. Much work remains to be done.

Guiding Questions

- What are your district's plans for professional-development activities?

- What organizational strategy has been implemented to support leadership and teacher development?

- How are district/school resources allocated to support a balanced professional-development strategy?

Chapter 7

Resources Acquisition:
Attention Required

"The money [in education] brings with it a tremendous bureaucracy that is far too busy with its own internal mechanics to produce results, or even to know when results are being achieved. They need only a few first-rate people to experiment, develop, learn, and demonstrate."

— Peter Drucker

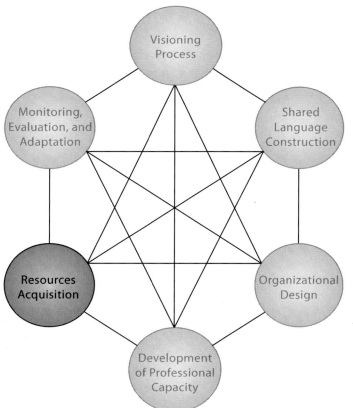

It is important that the acquisition of human and material resources be determined by a district or departmental plan. This is a matter of public trust. This plan is best described as the elements that constitute the *Organizational Inquiry Web*. The organizational design and district priorities (goals) resulting from the visioning process should be resourced in accordance with need. Whereas, in good economic times, social-service organizations often adopted the adage "More is better" when acquiring such resources, today's economy is very different. Effective budgetary practices necessarily are predicated upon systemic thinking, planning, and analysis. Ultimately, the learning organization should assess each budget request by asking: How is this particular request reflective of the departmental and organizational strategic plans? The answer to this question requires analysis and thoughtful collaboration. In the absence of such thoughtfulness, decision-makers will find themselves reacting to ever-changing budget realities, which can exert a significant impact upon the ability to maintain momentum toward declared goals. Organizational scale and adaptability should be kept in mind at all times.

The Human Element

A quality organization seeks well-qualified personnel. However, recruitment is not one-sided; a functional and integrated system will attract competent individuals. One of the leadership's primary responsibilities is the art of hiring the right people.

Jim Collins defines "the right people" as "those who are productively neurotic, self-motivated, and self-disciplined. These are the people who wake up every day compulsively driven to organizational and personal improvement." This quotation should be qualified by a statement that healthy employees are those who maintain an appropriate balance between their work and their personal lives. Such a balance is essential to ensuring their continued health and productivity.

Of course, attracting qualified employees requires clear vision of the desired attributes and skills. School districts are known to be bureaucratic and to vary widely in terms of their employees' competence, teaching styles, personalities, and motivations. The learning organization supports and embraces such diverse attributes. Research conducted by McKinsey on highest-rated schools concludes that the three factors most critical to student learning are: 1) hiring the right teachers; 2) developing their professional abilities; and 3) ensuring that district goals seek to secure the best possible instruction for every student. A good teacher's essential attributes include professional commitment, a superior work ethic, personal integrity, and a passion for student development. All other skills can be fostered through ongoing professional training.

The selection process is not always easy. This is especially true of public-schooling organizations, whose hiring practices are guided by collective agreements. However, an understanding of the district or departmental plan and of the hiring policies outlined by the collective agreements will serve to resolve most difficulties, as will working closely with a knowledgeable human-resources department. Once appropriate personnel has been hired, the leadership must determine which individuals are best suited for which roles. This, too, is an art. The successful accomplishment of this task increases the motivation, productivity, and commitment of teachers.

Since those holding school-based leadership positions (outside of collective agreements) are responsible for implementing the district's highest priorities, the following issues require careful consideration:

- Do existing processes encourage the recruitment of teachers as leaders whose skills align with the district's leadership vision?
- Which individuals within the organization are most qualified to hire future leaders?
- Which strategies promote leadership development that reflects the district's views concerning quality schools and student success?

The hiring process for both district- and school-leadership positions demands careful evaluation of the candidates' unique skill sets.

Resources and Budget

Public-schooling organizations must be able to respond to positive and to negative fiscal cycles. A negative budget cycle should not be used as an excuse to impede momentum toward declared goals. An essential component of a quality organization is the development of resourcing models built upon system analysis and equity parameters. One of the attributes of the *District/School Development Framework* as a planning tool is its scalability.

By using this combination of the *Universal Design for Learning* with the Components of Quality Schools as a guiding framework, leaders can create a focused, coherent, and systemic plan for development that may be adapted to changing budgets. In other words, this design will ensure that any change in school-district budgets will affect only the scale of the plan, but not its direction, focus, or declared commitments.

The following question often arises: Will professional-development expenditures for improving classroom-teacher practices reduce the need for other supports (such as for Education Assistants) over time? Yet learning organizations should not assume that proven staff-development initiatives will result in the reduction of other budgetary demands. Learning Forward contends:

> Professional learning may be viewed either as an investment that will pay future dividends on improved staff performance and student learning or [as] an expense that diminishes a school district's ability to meet its other financial obligations.

If a staff-development initiative is effective, and if it advances the district's ultimate purpose, it should be fully embraced. Sustainable resources should be budgeted accordingly. Only unproven or unsuccessful initiatives should be abandoned.

Our Development Journey

Acquiring suitable personnel and the necessary fiscal resources is predicated upon a coherent system-development strategy: *the strategic plan.* Such a plan can reduce significantly the difficulties encountered by district department-leaders during the budgeting and hiring processes. We believe that these processes demand the clarification of vision, the creation of a shared language, attention to organizational design, an understanding of how teachers impart knowledge and skills, and the elucidation of the district's role in school development.

As our departmental plan began to emerge, and later, as we sought to fill particular job positions, requisite employee attributes and skills proved easy to determine. Moreover, we noted almost immediately that experienced professionals were interested in our work. Never underestimate an organization's word-of-mouth! Qualified employees invariably are attracted to a vibrant environment that is infused with the directional momentum generated by a coherent plan.

Several other aspects of developmental structure also can provide momentum toward a declared goal. In addition to the scalable nature of our structural and conceptual organizational designs, the development of various staffing models has proven very helpful. These models provide for the allocation of Learner Support Teachers, Specialist Teachers, Counsellors, Education Assistants, and Child/ Youth Care Workers. The models are based upon system analysis incorporating equity parameters (e.g., inner-city schools, student demographics, and population totals), and allow for staffing varia-bility and for advocacy. These models also inform conversations about past and present staffing ratios when contemplating current budget realities and potential resourcing increases or reductions.

Our experience has taught us that, when committing to a strategic plan that incorporates promising practices, budgetary considerations will prove to be far less problematic and qualified professionals will find *you*.

Guiding Questions

- What strategies are implemented to ensure that qualified personnel are hired for the appropriate positions?

- What processes are established to ensure that budget requests align with the district or departmental plan?

- What systems or structures must be developed to ensure that district priorities are advanced, regardless of changing budgetary realities?

Chapter 8

Monitoring, Evaluation, and Adaptation: Determining Quality

"It is important to note that all indicators are flawed, whether qualitative or quantitative. What matters is not finding the perfect indicator, but settling upon a consistent and intelligent method of assessing your output results."

— Jim Collins

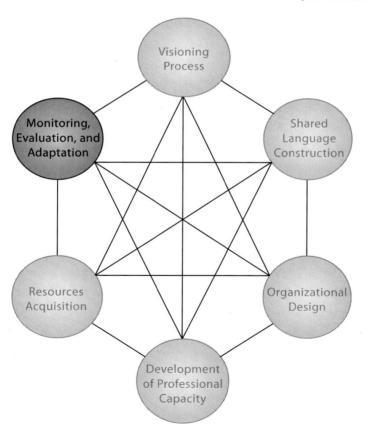

An organization is defined as a group of individuals working together toward common ends. The setting and adjustment of its direction are guided by: 1) clarity of organizational goals; and 2) evaluation of progress toward those goals. Such evaluation is essential as the systematic, evidence-based determination of worth, or quality. The evaluation of quality in business traditionally is determined by profit: the bottom line. The assessment of social services is more difficult, predicated largely upon the organization's responsiveness to legislative or social mandate. In social enterprises such as public schooling, too often quantitative assessment methods are used to measure quality. Therefore, it is imperative that district leaders devote the necessary time and energy to establish more holistic ways of evaluating schools and student learning. Not all things that are valuable can be quantified!

Empowering Professional Judgement

School districts often attempt to set direction and to assess system performance by adopting large-scale, one-dimensional quantitative measures. However, reliance upon such data as district-wide analysis of academic grades and standardized assessment results, without the filter of research-based best practices and relevant professional judgement, is not very helpful. District leaders are asked to use, to interpret, and to evaluate various sources of data and evidence in a particular context. Before they embark upon this process, insightful questions must be asked. As Tony Wagner asserts, "The real methodology for system change begins and ends with ongoing conversations about important questions." The leadership is responsible for the development and maintenance of an effective evaluation process.

Organizational Evaluation Cycle

Guided by research, we have developed an *Organizational Evaluation Cycle* that incorporates the interrelated elements of: 1) mandate clarification; 2) guiding questions; 3) data-collection methodology; 4) data compilation; 5) data interpretation; 6) response to guiding questions; and 7) goal-setting. This Cycle provides district leaders with a quality-assurance framework for implementation and reflection.

Elements of the Organizational Evaluation Cycle

Mandate Clarification
Mandate clarification is a key aspect of an organization's visioning process. In public-schooling organizations, the mandate is derived from the legislative imperatives that define the roles of districts, schools, principals, and teachers (for instance, the *British Columbia School Act*). Mandate clarification requires that leaders review relevant legislation and that they convey and reinforce the system's core purposes.

Guiding Questions
Guiding questions spring from a well-defined mandate, allowing leaders to develop a core set of questions about organizational goals and evaluation processes.

Data-collection Methodology
Data-collection methodology entails assembling pertinent data in order to give a knowledgeable response to each of the guiding questions. The data collected may be quantitative, qualitative, or both.

Data Compilation
Data compilation refers to the process of organizing and refining data that addresses the guiding questions. The organization of data is an important step in enabling efficient and successful decision-making.

Data Interpretation
Data interpretation is the process by which the leadership reviews data in relation to the guiding questions. This includes analysis, discussion, and a synthesis of the data, which is filtered through shared professional judgement.

Response to Guiding Questions

Once the collected data has been interpreted and organizational leaders have expressed their views, a report of these findings and conclusions will serve to answer the Guiding Questions. These answers, in turn, will faciliate an evaluation of the organization's status and progress with regard to the mandate.

Goal-setting

Goal-setting is the process of adjusting current organizational goals according to the responses to guiding questions.

Our Development Journey

Several years ago, our senior leadership team hosted a week-long district review, conducted by the Ministry of Education. This review examined the district strategies and structures that were designed to promote quality schooling. The following questions guided conversations throughout the week: 1) How does your district define and evaluate "quality schools"?; and 2) What strategy does your district employ when a school is determined to be in need of assistance? These questions were a significant catalyst for the writing of this book. We left the meetings pondering a means of developing a system-wide definition of a "quality school" and of establishing what evidence would support such a conclusion.

We also researched what actions would be required at the district level to promote quality schools. The systemic approach presented here enables schools and district personnel to engage in an inquiry-based development process.

Our approach is designed to confront the challenging issues of monitoring, evaluation, and adaptation. Some of these activities require a shared understanding of objective data and of subjective evidence types, as well as definitions of quality and of the need for improvement. These issues, representing some of the district leadership's chief concerns, demand the collective wisdom of experienced professionals.

The *Organizational Evaluation Cycle* provides real-time evidence and information to leadership about how well schools are meeting their goals. Additionally, it identifies which areas merit future development. The Evaluation Cycle does not suggest blame; rather, it encourages continuous engagement and reflection regarding the core area of focus.

We are convinced that engagement and reflection are essential to growth. When improvement is assessed, in part, by rendering guiding beliefs as questions, these questions serve to identify to the leadership the necessary next steps. For example, how have our actions built capacity at the classroom level? Without such direction, and in the absence of guiding beliefs to maintain a focus upon the organization's highest priorities, all opinions and ideas about school improvement tend to be regarded as equal. Yet research and practice clearly indicate that all opinions and ideas are *not* equal.

It is important to remember that the elements of the *Organizational Evaluation Cycle* demand continual reflection. Senior leaders are responsible for monitoring quality, and constituents need to be confident that every public school is engaged in ensuring the best possible education for every student.

Guiding Questions

- How does district leadership define and assess "quality schooling"?

- What structures are necessary at the district level in order to advance school development?

- What data and other information sources should be used to assess progress in school development and to guide district actions?

Organizational Inquiry Rubric

"A rubric is a particular format for criteria — it is a written-down version of the criteria. The best rubrics are worded in a way that covers the essence of what [organizational leaders] look for when they judge quality, and they reflect the best thinking in the field about what constitutes good performance."

— Arter & McTighe

The following Rubric, based upon our leadership experience and research, is designed to provide a condensed version of the *Organizational Inquiry Web*. Examples are organized on a continuum of **Attention Required, Promising Practices,** and **Optimal Functioning,** and correspond with each interrelated element of the *Organizational Inquiry Web*. We trust it will provide you with additional, practical guidance in developing and sustaining a vibrant learning organization.

Your own blank copy of the *Organizational Inquiry Rubric* is available for printing at www.edusystems.ca .

Systemic Organizational Health	Attention Required	Promising Practices	Optimal Functioning
Visioning Process	Leadership is unclear regarding one or more elements of the visioning process (mandate, vision, guiding beliefs, goal-setting). Core purpose and values are unclear, and consequently have limited impact upon directional focus. The "big picture" either is not clearly articulated or appears to employees to be in a constant state of change.	Leadership has a plan to address the interconnected elements of mandate, vision, guiding beliefs, and goal-setting. Core purpose and values are articulated, and exert impact upon directional focus; the "big picture" is becoming clearer. There is emerging alignment between the visioning process, organization goals, and practices.	Leadership is engaged in the interactive, collaborative, and dynamic visioning process, inclusive of mandate clarification, vision creation, guiding beliefs development, and goal-setting. Core purpose and values inform organizational architecture, sustain directional focus, and illuminate the "big picture" for all employees. There is a culture of commitment to the organizational direction, demonstrated by the translation of ideology into action (e.g., goals, strategies, procedures).
Shared Language Construction	There is little evidence of the development of organizational maxims or of procedural language. Employees expend significant time and energy in attempting to clarify mandate and processes, which limits their ability to focus upon problem-solving. Technology is not utilized strategically to disseminate procedural language.	Organizational maxims exist, but are not used to inform the organizational narrative. Procedural language exists, but with limited continuity or alignment across the organization (e.g., across departments). Technology is used on a limited basis to disseminate procedural language.	Guiding beliefs and problem-solving methods are influenced by the development and strategic articulation of two types of shared language: 1) organizational maxims; and 2) procedural language. The organization effectively uses technology (online repository) to maintain and to support the broad-based dissemination of procedural language.

Systemic Organizational Health	Attention Required	Promising Practices	Optimal Functioning
Organizational Design	Alignment between the organizational purpose and design is not immediately apparent. The organizational design does not appear to support the development of multidisciplinary teams. Professional-development activities appear to be isolated and not linked to a systemic plan.	The organizational design is aligned, to some extent, with the visioning process. There is recognition that multidisciplinary teams support knowledge transfer, even if the system's architecture lacks coherent organization. The organization has not yet developed a structural plan to support ongoing professional development.	The organizational design is clearly aligned with the visioning process. The organizational design or architecture promotes: 1) multidisciplinary teams; 2) flexible boundaries; 3) a professional culture committed to a balance between relationships and results; and 4) the exchange or transfer of innovative ideas. The organization is committed to ongoing professional learning, and has a clear strategy that supports a continuum of professional-development activities connected to key research.
Development of Professional Capacity	While professional-development opportunities are provided, there is limited evidence of a strategic plan to foster employee development.	Leadership is committed to the improvement of individuals throughout the organization. Ongoing professional-development activities are provided. There is an awareness that professional development should reflect research findings and should be developed over time.	The learning organization continually demonstrates its commitment to the professional development of all employees. Professional-development activities are inspired by research regarding how employees convert new knowledge and skills into practice. A professional-development continuum, based upon research on: 1) staff development; and 2) student engagement/ learning, is actively being implemented.

Systemic Organizational Health	Attention Required	Promising Practices	Optimal Functioning
Resources Acquisition	Hiring practices are predominately focused upon seniority. The acquisition of human and material resources frequently is determined by the view that "More is better." Hiring and development of leaders does not appear to be guided by an overarching vision on the part of the leadership.	There are established criteria in place for all staffing roles throughout the organization, with thoughtful processes and support for employee selection. Leadership reviews all resource requests as they pertain to departmental plans, organizational goals, and budget realities. The hiring and development of leaders is regarded as an important responsibility.	There is a demonstrated commitment to the acquisition of human resources. Budgeted human and material resources clearly are connected to an overarching and collaboratively developed scalable plan that incorporates staffing models. The hiring and development of leaders is systematic and aligns with the district's highest priorities.
Monitoring, Evaluation, and Adaptation	Leadership is aware of its responsibility in the evaluation process, but is fragmented in its approach to gathering appropriate data and to analyzing results to determine system actions.	Leadership recognizes its responsibility for the development and maintenance of an authentic evaluation process. Leadership is working to generate an evaluation method that will indicate any needed system improvements.	Leadership has developed, and has articulated clearly, an ongoing organizational evaluation cycle. To guide the evaluation process, leadership has identified key questions related to guiding beliefs and to the clarity of organizational goals. A successful evaluation process has been devised that reflects research, collaboration, system utility, and the leadership's professional judgement.

Chapter 9

Organizational Coherence: Interpersonal and Structural Elements

Part I: Interpersonal Elements

"Growing diversity of the population and workforce [has] forced a reorientation toward an open-systems mindset ... as part of a complex, interconnected whole."

— Richard Daft

Healthy organizations accomplish the following objectives: 1) increase employee motivation and sense of belonging; 2) promote continuous learning and innovation; 3) attract competent practitioners; and 4) improve outcomes and results.

Professional Relationships

By striving to ensure that all interactions among stakeholders are personally, professionally, and mutually beneficial, healthy organizations consistently reinforce a "Take the high road" approach that is based upon established trust and transparency. Leaders would be wise to avoid the development of adversarial dynamics that pit one person or stakeholder group against another. Frequently, time, money, and energy are wasted in fending off mistrust, hurt feelings, and potential litigation. Instead, when strongly held positions appear to be incompatible, the crucial elements of problem-solving should be employed: listening in order to understand; clarifying roles, responsibilities, and values; and maintaining a respectful demeanour at all times.

Interpersonal Interactions

A culture that embraces the open exchange of divergent ideas will prove to be a vibrant and productive workplace. A leader's commitment to respectful modes of communication will leave no place for sarcasm, belittling remarks, or inappropriate, demeaning interactions.

Talk Less; Listen More

An awareness of group dynamics should prompt all responsible leaders to participate mainly by listening attentively. The best results are obtained when leaders *contribute* to, but do not direct the exchange of, creative ideas between group members.

Flow of Communication

Effective communication should flow freely between the various organizational departments and entities. A respectful leader carefully composes each message and chooses its method of delivery (e.g., face-to-face, large meeting, corporate memo). Since employees value a sense of involvement in the workplace, a personal approach generally is recommended.

Trust

Leaders are expected to nurture their employees' potential. By demonstrating a genuine trust in their staff members, and by regarding them as self-motivated professionals, leaders will create an environment that encourages and inspires innovation. Only in a climate of trust can learning organizations enable both individuals and the collective to grow and to flourish.

Encouragement

A healthy organization encourages and celebrates its employees' efforts, commitments, innovations, and successes. Since educators work in public service, a field that often goes without acknowledgement, leaders should be aware that a well-timed word or token of appreciation will contribute greatly toward motivating and inspiring their staff. Although no year-end bonuses are given in the public-school system, recognition may be expressed with a card, a book or other gift, or a public tribute. These expressions of gratitude are important.

Care and Concern

Leaders should demonstrate a genuine concern for workplace safety and a respect for the personal life challenges of all employees. This includes recognition of the grief suffered by any group member upon the loss of a loved one. It should be signaled clearly to all staff that this is an organization that cares about the individual.

Dignified Support

When an employee is struggling with performance expectations or similar issues, a thoughtful leader will provide discreet support that does not compromise that person's dignity. However, even sensitive situations require immediate intervention if harm is being done to another individual or group. A helpful intervention and support model is based upon established values and addresses these key questions:

- What issue is the employee struggling with?
- Who or what is affected by these struggles?
- Does the resultant situation require immediate intervention?
- What kind of support is appropriate for this individual?

Suitable intervention and support for an individual in need may benefit the entire organization.

Part II: Structural Elements

"Quality is the result of a carefully constructed environment. It has to be the fabric of the organization — not part of the fabric."

— Philip Crosby

Healthy organizations consciously strive to develop structural elements that are respectful of, and beneficial to, all stakeholders. These structural components are designed to promote a positive work culture, to inculcate a relentless commitment to stated purposes, and to foster a quality organization.

Recognizing Diversity
Representative diversity in leadership is essential to sustained success. Effective leaders recognize that diversity offers a richness of opinion and of perspective within the organization, while also cultivating an inclusive, nurturing environment.

Twenty-first-century globalization places an increased responsibility upon public schooling to model how society should view diversity. At the same time, public schooling demonstrates that we all can live and learn together.

Supporting Leadership
Organizations must support their leadership through system structures and through direct communication. Yet one must be aware of the potential consequences of inadvertently undermining leaders by means of the very initiatives intended to offer assistance. A balance must be preserved between appropriate leadership consultation and aid, and the institutionalizing of inadequacy. All

communication and consultation regarding leadership should address the following questions:

- Who is best qualified to make this decision?
- What are the potential negative consequences of excluding this individual from the decision-making process?

Decision-making

Decision-making often is defined as the process of identifying and solving problems. However, there are decisions that need to be made in an organization even before any problems can be resolved. Few organizations delineate individual roles in the decision-making process; they fail to stipulate who is expected to make which decisions. Yet the establishment of, and adherence to, an understanding of respective roles will generate the following results: 1) the empowerment of appropriate personnel and the facilitation of action; 2) less role confusion; 3) a natural accountability; and 4) appropriate advocacy.

Exceptional decision-makers appear to have an innate capacity to: 1) identify a problem or a lack of direction; 2) obtain necessary information and observations from the relevant people; 3) integrate information into a coherent statement of the problem; 4) determine the appropriate course of action; and 5) implement the decision.

This process results from asking the right questions.

Decision-making — A Problem-solving Format:

- What is the problem?
- Whose problem is it?
- What is the cause of the problem?
- What can be done to remedy this situation?

- Have I/we considered a range of possible solutions?
- Did intervention resolve the problem?

A recognition that each decision made affects future decisions should serve to align a chosen course of action with the overarching organizational plan.

Collaboration

Collaborative decision-making is an organizational necessity. Whenever practicable, leadership should consult the affected individual(s) or stakeholder group(s) in any decision or implementation of change. A collaborative dynamic conveys the message that all opinions in the work environment are valued and respected.

Territorialism

Learning organizations expect leaders to align support structures so as to ensure the best possible outcomes. However, such alignment may result in a partial overlapping of responsibilities, and some affected individuals may resist any integration of departments or duties. Clearly, this opposition must be addressed. Conversely, dedicated members of the organization will welcome the efficiency of aligned, coherent, and sustainable structures.

Meetings

The several potential meeting configurations serve various purposes that determine their respective designs (environment) and structures (procedures). Consideration of a meeting's environment includes elements such as venue, number and titles of participants, seating arrangements, and requisite technology. Procedures encompass a meeting's format, topics, duration, and style of presentation. Attention to these elements will yield efficient meetings and productive communication.

Advisory and Advocacy Groups

Key constituents provide valuable information. These advisory and advocacy groups include students, parents, teachers, administrators, the Aboriginal community, and Special Needs advocacy groups. All contribute to the constructive exchange of ideas and to a successful decision-making process. Consequently, the participation of these stakeholder groups is sought on a continual basis.

Supporting Innovative Thinking

A quality public-schooling organization recognizes that the benefits of fostering innovation exceed even their impact upon student learning. Innovators inspire and motivate improvement throughout the learning organization's culture; therefore, the organization should encourage its innovators.

To this end, learning laboratories may be instituted to promote the pursuit of creative practices. These laboratories enhance the organization and its image, while also affording other practitioners concrete, observable examples of pioneering best practices for improvement.

Organizational Coherence Reflection Tool

"Meaningful, reflective conversations can sustain and nourish us. They can raise individual and collective consciousness. Above all else, they involve a discussion of values. This is at the heart of the improvement process."

— Ghaye & Ghaye

This chart enables individuals or groups to assess their organization's current standing with respect to the continuum comprised of **Attention Required, Promising Practice**, and **Optimal Functioning**. The corresponding areas of focus, Part I: Interpersonal Elements and Part II: Structural Elements, consist of the terms previously described, and are essential to organizational coherence and quality.

This assessment tool is intended for reflection purposes only.

Your own blank copy of the *Organizational Coherence Reflection Tool* is available for printing at www.edusystems.ca .

Organizational Coherence	Attention Required	Promising Practices	Optimal Functioning
Professional Relationships Leaders demonstrate a commitment to interpersonal interaction based upon trust and honesty.	☐	☐	☐
Leaders avoid adversarial dynamics with individuals and stakeholder groups.	☐	☐	☐
Interpersonal Interactions Leaders create an emotionally safe environment for staff.	☐	☐	☐
Leaders foster a culture that encourages the thoughtful exchange of ideas.	☐	☐	☐
Talk Less; Listen More Leaders demonstrate an understanding of their influences upon group dynamics.	☐	☐	☐
Flow of Communication Leaders demonstrate a commitment to the effective flow of communication throughout the organization.	☐	☐	☐
Trust Leaders demonstrate belief and confidence in all staff members.	☐	☐	☐
Leaders encourage, motivate, and inspire, by fostering mutual trust.	☐	☐	☐
Encouragement Leaders seek ways to celebrate successes and to encourage staff members, both individually and collectively.	☐	☐	☐
Care and Concern Leaders demonstrate genuine concern for staff welfare.	☐	☐	☐
Dignified Support Leaders actively support any struggling staff members discreetly and without judgement.	☐	☐	☐

Organizational Coherence	Attention Required	Promising Practices	Optimal Functioning
Recognizing Diversity Leaders value diversity as a source of richness of opinion and of perspective.	☐	☐	☐
Supporting Leadership Leaders make appropriate decisions, in accordance with the best ways to support other leaders at various levels of the organization.	☐	☐	☐
Decision-making Leaders clarify each person's role in any decisions. Leaders demonstrate clear decision-making processes that reflect the overarching plan.	☐ ☐	☐ ☐	☐ ☐
Collaboration Leaders demonstrate a commitment to collaborative decision-making. Leaders show respect for divergent opinions.	☐ ☐	☐ ☐	☐ ☐
Territorialism Leaders align support structures to enable improved outcomes rather than to accommodate individual preferences. Leaders address any resistance to collaboration.	☐ ☐	☐ ☐	☐ ☐
Meetings Leaders demonstrate respect for staff by planning meetings with clear purposes.	☐	☐	☐
Advisory and Advocacy Groups Leaders welcome contributions from various stakeholder groups. Leaders seek opportunities to incorporate ideas introduced by advisory and advocacy groups.	☐ ☐	☐ ☐	☐ ☐
Supporting Innovative Thinking Leaders encourage innovation that fosters system development.	☐	☐	☐

Chapter 10

The Professional Teacher:
Rights and Responsibilities

Seek truth, create, and live up to the title of teacher.

— Motto of East China Normal University, Shanghai

A professional teacher possesses the knowledge and skills to design both the instruction and the environment for enhanced learning by all students. Pillars of teaching practice include: 1) curriculum design; 2) instructional technique; 3) quality assessment and evaluation practices; 4) extensive content knowledge; 5) appreciation of student developmental readiness and interests; and 6) management of the learning environment.

The mastery of these and of related skills requires a career-long developmental process that integrates technique with the practitioner's own personality. Indeed, Parker Palmer asserts that good teaching cannot be reduced to technique; rather, it is the result of the convergence of identity and integrity. In other words, we teach who we are.

A teacher's implied contract with the public accords him or her a degree of autonomy and self-determination in return for an agreement that public interests will be placed above those of the individual (as stated by the British Columbia College of Teachers).

In public schooling, teachers have certain rights to professional autonomy, or more specifically, to the self-determination to exercise their professional judgement with regard to curriculum and to instructional and assessment strategies. They are expected to possess technical subject knowledge, a deep understanding of developmental psychology, and a dedication to the pillars of pedagogy.

A teacher's autonomy is predicated upon the knowledge of: 1) statute law (e.g., *School Act*); 2) prescribed learning outcomes (e.g., Ministry of Education); and 3) the duties and responsibilities stipulated by the employer (e.g., School Board Policy). Professional autonomy generally is guided by the pertinent regulatory body (e.g., the College of Teachers), which monitors membership and which describes the expected standards of practice. Additionally, the College of Teachers defines public schooling's standards of ethical conduct, while the *School Act* defines teachers' legal duties.

Teachers are required to master a well-defined area of expertise, to make independent decisions that evince high standards of competence and of conduct, and to devote themselves to ongoing, collaborative professional learning and skills development. In his book *After Theory*, Terry Eagleton declares:

> Professional autonomy should not be taken to mean
> teachers exercising professional judgement in isolation
> from their peers, but rather that they develop their pro-
> fessional learning through systematic investigation ...

Successful learning organizations recognize the threefold benefits of systemic professional development: 1) the fostering of a vibrant professional community; 2) improved, system-wide instructional practices; and 3) the enhancement of public confidence in the profession. District- and school-based leadership must create these opportunities for teachers' professional growth. This is a shared responsibility.

Chapter 11

School-based Leadership:
The Key to Success

"The more complex society gets, the more sophisticated leadership must become."

— Michael Fullan

Public-school principals and vice principals are entrusted with substantial duties and responsibilities, as defined in: 1) law or legislation (e.g., *School Act*, Child Abuse Reporting law, Criminal Code, *Freedom of Information and Protection of Privacy Act*); 2) Ministry of Education policies and procedures; 3) school board policies and regulations; 4) codes of professional practice; and 5) inter-agency protocols. Among these obligations are instructional leadership, business management, budgeting, ensuring safe and caring learning environments, emergency preparedness and response, human-resources and staff development, school planning, community liaison, coach, teacher, mentor, and mediator.

A meta-analysis spanning thirty-five years reveals the effects of school principals' values, decisions, and actions upon staff development and student learning. In the book *School Leadership That Works: From Research to Results*, authors Marzano, Waters, and McNulty include a quotation from the 1977 U.S. Senate Select Committee Report on Equal Educational Opportunity:

In many ways, the school principal is the most important individual in any school. If the school is a vibrant, innovative, child-centered place, if it has a reputation for excellence in teaching, if students are performing to the best of their ability, one can almost always point to the principal's leadership as a key to success.

In the complex milieu of public schooling, it is important that there be a clear understanding of a principal's mandated duties, as opposed to the negotiable aspects of his or her job. The mandatory functions, which are non-negotiable, encompass the above-mentioned legal, legislative, and policy-related requirements of educational governance. The negotiable aspects of a school leader's work focus primarily upon the development of a dynamic school culture for all stakeholders. This goal includes the fostering of teachers' professional growth, in order to enhance student engagement, learning, and success.

Principals and vice principals also should have a comprehensive grasp of collective agreements as they pertain to managerial rights and to teachers' rights, responsibilities, and autonomy.

Although leadership development constitutes an integral part of a school district's plan for improvement, such initiatives alone cannot guarantee progress. School districts should incorporate district-level consultation, to assist school principals and vice principals in achieving their objectives. The *District/School Development Framework* and other components of the *Organizational Inquiry Web* detailed in this text offer consultation models that facilitate the collaborative design of coherent, sustainable plans for professional development.

Because of the limits placed upon formal authority, principals and vice principals may exert influence to effect desired change by means of persuasion and the fostering of shared commitment. Integrity and dedication are essential prerequisites for a selfless "can do" attitude that engenders trust and inspires enthusiasm.

The ability to motivate employees is indispensable. Nonetheless, relationship-building should not eclipse a leader's equally important focus upon the attainment of specific results. As Michael Fullan states:

> ... Relationships are crucial, but only if they work at the hard task of establishing greater program coherence ... The role of leadership is to cause greater capacity throughout the organization in order to get better results (learning).

Thus, while a school's success is predicated to a large extent upon its leadership, effective school leadership, in turn, is founded upon a balance between relationships and a results orientation.

Chapter 12

The Limits of Public Schooling:
A Shared Responsibility

It takes a whole village to raise a child.

— African Proverb

Clearly, a well-educated person is not solely the product of public schooling or of other academic institutions; family, community, and government all play significant roles in his or her development. Thus, we regard public education as a communal responsibility. Yet, all too often, public schooling is seen as the remedy for society and consequently becomes the target of criticism when aspirations for our children are not realized. While public schooling struggles to meet expectations, Abbott observes:

> ... Home and community have been weakened as government has expanded the role of the school, effectively creating a whole new generation of overschooled but undereducated young people.

Since the mid-twentieth century, Western societies have undergone a continual and fundamental transformation of social paradigms and institutions. Gender roles and relationships (with regard to identity, sexuality, and family), political and social structures, and the nature of personal and communal belonging are all being redefined.

Manuel Castells argues that we are in a " ... historic period of destructuring of organizations, delegitimization of institutions, and the fading of major social movements ... " He contends that this is contributing to a postmodern culture that:

> ... indulges in celebrating the end of history, and, to some extent, the end of reason, giving up the capacity to understand ... The implicit assumption is the acceptance of full individualization of behaviour, and of society's powerlessness over its destiny.

The quest for individualization may lead to societal polarization, expressed either as ideological fanaticism or as selfish indifference. Such intolerance and insularity represent the antithesis of the reasoned, respectful, and non-judgemental attitude necessary to sustain a pluralistic society.

While social paradigms and institutions are being reformulated, the larger community expects public schooling to fill the gap and to remedy many real or perceived social ills. Families, communities, and the government itself, although in many cases no longer embracing either their own or shared responsibilities, demand that students achieve optimal results and hold schools "accountable" for disappointing outcomes. Ironically, of course, the schools' additional responsibilities serve to underscore the societal failings that inevitably hinder students' ability to meet their own expectations or the needs of a restructured, democratic society.

Paul Monroe expresses the prominent role that academic institutions are expected to play:

> ... to transmit to each succeeding generation the elements of culture and institutional life that have been found to be of value in the past, and that additional increment of culture which the existing generation has succeeded in working out for itself, to do this and also [to] give each individual the fullest liberty in formulating his [or her] own aims in life and in shaping his [or her] own activities to these purposes.

All democratic societies are guided by similar declarations, which inspire responsible citizenry and representative government alike. For example, in Canada, the culture toward which we aspire is outlined by the *Canadian Charter of Rights and Freedoms*. As traditional institutions such as family, community, and church undergo radical change, it is hardly surprising that increasing demands are made upon public schooling.

During this process of transformation, the vision of a democratic society (incorporating pluralism, religious freedom, and responsible citizenry and government) demands that its members possess the mediating tools of reason, adaptability, and tolerance. As Abbott observes:

> ... Democracy depends upon being respectful of other people's ideas both in public and in private, for our real authority comes from our personal example of living together within an interdependent community.

Alexis de Tocqueville addressed these same ideals almost two hundred years ago when he declared that "the first duty imposed on those who now direct society is to educate democracy; to put, if possible new life into its beliefs ... ."

Nonetheless, some of the host of expectations now placed at the doorstep of public schooling are misguided and unattainable. Yet public schools must be held partially responsible for not having communicated clearly or having established appropriate boundaries. All stakeholders should commit themselves, once again, to sustaining our country's idealism concerning public schooling. As John Dewey notes in his book *Experiences & Education*:

> It would not be a sign of health if such an important social interest as education were not also an arena of struggles, practical and theoretical ... It is the business of an intelligent theory of education to ascertain the causes for the conflicts that exist and then, instead of taking one side or the other, to indicate a plan of operations proceeding from a level deeper and more inclusive than is represented by the practices and ideas of the contending parties.

This is an apt demonstration of democracy: the resolve to seek communal solutions.

Afterword

"We cannot afford to indulge in a sophomoric skepticism that absolves us of the responsibility to look at and act on information that tells us how well ... [or how badly] we are doing ...

— Rick Stiggins

We believe that the formulation and writing of one's philosophical position is an essential precondition for testing and debating ideas in the public arena. John Stuart Mill embraces this collective forum in his text *On Liberty and Other Essays*:

> If there are any persons who contest a received opinion
> ... let us thank them for it, open our minds to listen to
> them, and rejoice that there is [someone] to do for us
> what we otherwise ought, if we have any regard for the
> certainty or vitality of our conviction, to do with much
> greater labor for ourselves.

Since system development entails significant challenges, conflicting opinions on its method of implementation in public schooling are to be expected. However, when system leaders are familiar with research findings and with seminal thinking, such challenges can be reframed as opportunities.

The proposed synthesis of organizational-design principles and teacher-development initiatives provides a practical resource that will improve engagement and outcomes for public-school students, teachers, and leadership system-wide. We invite all professional educators and system leaders to reflect critically upon the important issues examined within these pages.

Resources

The Role of Public Schooling: From Its Roots to the Present

Abbott, John, "A Briefing Paper for Parliamentarians on the Design Faults at the Heart of English Education." *The 21st Century Learning Initiative*. Aug. 2009. Online.

Bacon, Francis. *Novum Organum*. 1620. Chicago: Carus, 1999. Print.

Bricker, Darrell and Edward Greenspon. *Searching for Certainty: Inside the Canadian Mindset*. Canada: Doubleday, 2001. Print.

Flyvbjerg, Bent. *Making Social Science Matter: Why Social Inquiry Fails and How it Can Succeed Again*. New York: Cambridge University Press, 2001. Print.

Hargreaves, Andy. *Teaching in the Knowledge Society: Education in the Age of Insecurity*. New York: Teachers College Press, 2003. Print.

Monroe, Paul. *A Brief Course in the History of Education*. London: MacMillan, 1918. Print.

Palmer, Parker J. *The Courage to Teach: Exploring the Inner Landscape of a Teacher's Life*. New York: Jossey-Bass, 1998. Print.

Paul, Richard W. *Critical Thinking: How to Prepare for a Rapidly Changing World*. Santa Rosa: Foundation for Critical Thinking, 1995. Print.

Robinson, Ken. *The Element: How Finding Your Passion Changes Everything*. New York: Viking, 2009. Print.

Stewart, Douglas. *"Purposes of Public Education: Philosophical Reflections." Education Canada*, Vol. 45, No. 1. Toronto: Canadian Education Association, 2005. Print.

Systemic Thinking: Essential to Success

Argyris, Chris and Donald. A. Schön. *Organizational Learning II: Theory, Method, and Practice*. New York: Addison-Wesley, 1996. Print.

Bennett, William. J., Chester E. Finn Jr., and John T. E. Cribb Jr. *The Educated Child: A Parent's Guide from Preschool through Eighth Grade*. New York: Free Press, 1999. Print.

Collins, Jim. *Good to Great and the Social Sectors: A Monograph to Accompany Good to Great*. HarperCollins, 2005. Print.

Fullan, Michael. *Change Forces: Probing the Depths of Educational Reform*. London: Falmer Press, 1992. Print.

Marzano, Robert J. and Timothy Waters. *District Leadership That Works: Striking the Right Balance*. Bloomington: Solution Tree, 2009. Print.

Ryan, P. G. "*A Case Study of A Networked Learning Community: 'The Third Space.'*" Diss. University of British Columbia, 2009. Print.

Sarason, Seymour B. *The Predictable Failure of School Reform: Can We Change Course Before It's Too Late?* San Francisco: Jossey-Bass, 1990. Print.

Schlechty, Phillip C. *Inventing Better Schools: An Action Plan for Educational Reform.* San Francisco: Jossey-Bass, 1997. Print.

Senge, Peter M. *The Fifth Discipline: The Art and Practice of the Learning Organization.* New York: Doubleday, 1990. Print.

Wiens, J. R. and D. Coulter. "What is an educated Canadian?" *Education Canada*, Vol. 45, No. 1. 2005. Print.

The Visioning Process: The Journey Begins

Collins, James C. and Jerry I. Porras. *Built to Last: Successful Habits of Visionary Companies.* New York: HarperCollins, 2002. Print.

Collins, Jim. *Good to Great and the Social Sectors: A Monograph to Accompany Good to Great.* HarperCollins, 2005. Print.

Drucker, Peter F. and Joseph A. Maciariello. *Management.* New York: HarperCollins, 2008. Print.

Shared Language Construction: From Vision to Action

Hildreth, Paul and Chris Kimble. *Knowledge Networks: Innovation Through Communities of Practice*. London: Idea, 2004. Print.

Lazaridou, Angeliki. "The Kinds of Knowledge Principals Use: Implications for Training." *International Journal of Education Policy and Leadership*, Vol. 4, No. 10. Oct. 2009. Print.

Nonaka, Ikujiro. "A Dynamic Theory of Organizational Knowledge Creation." *Organization Science*, Vol. 5, No. 1. Feb. 1994. Print.

Organizational Design: Form Follows Function

Cole, Robert W. *Educating Everybody's Children: Diverse Teaching Strategies for Diverse Learners: What Research and Practice Say about Improving Achievement*. Alexandria: ASCD, 1995. Print.

Gordon, D., J. Gravel, and L. Schifter. *A Policy Reader in Universal Design for Learning*. Cambridge: Harvard Press, 2009. Print.

Marzano, Robert J. and Timothy Waters. *District Leadership That Works: Striking the Right Balance*. Bloomington: Solution Tree, 2009. Print.

National Staff Development Council. *Standards for Staff Development: Advancing Student Learning Through Staff Development*. 2001. Print.

Preskill, Hallie and Rosalie T. Torres. *Evaluative Inquiry for Learning in Organizations*. Thousand Oaks: Sage, 1999. Print.

Rose, D., A. Meyer, N. Strangman, and G. Rappolt. *Teaching Every Student in the Digital Age: Universal Design for Learning.* Alexandria: ASCD, 2002. Print.

Schlechty, Phillip C. *Inventing Better Schools: An Action Plan for Educational Reform.* San Francisco: Jossey-Bass, 1997. Print.

Schmoker, Mike. *Results: The Key to Continuous School Improvement.* Alexandria: ASCD, 1999. Print.

Supovitz, Jonathan. "Why We Need District-Based Reform: Supporting System-Wide Instructional Improvement." *Education Week*, Vol. 27, Is. 13. Nov. 2007. Print.

Wang, Margaret. C., Geneva D. Haertel and Herbert. J. Walberg. "Toward a Knowledge Base for School Learning." *Review of Educational Research*, Vol. 63, No. 3. 1993. Print.

Development of Professional Capacity: Fostering Student Engagement

Aalst, Hans. "Networking in Society, Organizations and Education." *Schooling for Tomorrow: Networks of Innovation Towards New Models for Managing Schools and Systems.* Paris: OECD Publications, 2003. Print.

Abbott, John, "A Briefing Paper for Parliamentarians on the Design Faults at the Heart of English Education." *The 21st Century Learning Initiative.* August 2009. Online.

Argyris, Chris and Donald. A. Schön. *Organizational Learning II: Theory, Method, and Practice.* New York: Addison-Wesley, 1996. Print.

Cheetham, Graham. and Geoff Chivers. *Professions, Competence and Informal Learning.* Northampton: Edward Elgar, 2005. Print.

Dreyfus, Hubert L. and Stuart E. Dreyfus. *Mind Over Machine: The Power of Human Intuition and Expertise in the Era of the Computer.* New York: Free Press, 1988. Print.

Earl, L. and S. Katz. "What makes a network a learning network?" *National College for School Leadership.* 2005. Online.

Gordon, D., J. Gravel, and L. Schifter. *A Policy Reader in Universal Design for Learning.* Cambridge: Harvard Press, 2009. Print.

Joyce, Bruce and Showers, Beverly. "Improving Inservice Training: The Message of Research." *Educational Leadership*, Vol. 37, No. 5. Feb. 1980. Print.

Marzano, Robert J. and Timothy Waters. *District Leadership That Works: Striking the Right Balance.* Bloomington: Solution Tree, 2009. Print.

National Staff Development Council. *Standards for Staff Development: Advancing Student Learning Through Staff Development.* 2001. Print.

Protheroe, Nancy. "NCLB Dismisses Research Vital to Effective Teaching." *Education Digest*, Vol. 69, No. 8. Apr. 2004. Print.

Robinson, Ken. *The Element: How Finding Your Passion Changes Everything.* New York: Viking, 2009. Print.

Supovitz, Jonathan. "Why We Need District-Based Reform: Supporting System-Wide Instructional Improvement." *Education Week*, Vol. 27, Is. 13. Nov. 2007. Print.

Resources Acquisition: Attention Required

Collins, Jim. *Good to Great and the Social Sectors: A Monograph to Accompany Good to Great.* HarperCollins, 2005. Print.

Drucker, Peter F. and Joseph A. Maciariello. *Management.* New York: HarperCollins, 2008. Print.

Marzano, Robert J. and Timothy Waters. *District Leadership That Works: Striking the Right Balance.* Bloomington: Solution Tree, 2009. Print.

McKinsey & Company. *How the Best Performing School Systems Come Out On Top.* New York: McKinsey & Company, 2007. Print.

National Staff Development Council. *Standards for Staff Development: Advancing Student Learning Through Staff Development.* 2001. Print.

Monitoring, Evaluation, and Adaptation: Determining Quality

Collins, Jim. *Good to Great and the Social Sectors: A Monograph to Accompany Good to Great.* HarperCollins, 2005. Print.

National Staff Development Council. *Standards for Staff Development: Advancing Student Learning Through Staff Development.* 2001. Print.

Preskill, Hallie and Rosalie T. Torres. *Evaluative Inquiry for Learning in Organizations*. Thousand Oaks: Sage, 1999. Print.

Schlechty, Phillip C. *Inventing Better Schools: An Action Plan for Educational Reform*. San Francisco: Jossey-Bass, 1997. Print.

Schmoker, Mike. *Results: The Key to Continuous School Improvement*. Alexandria: ASCD, 1999. Print.

Wagner, Tony. *The Global Achievement Gap: Why Even Our Best Schools Don't Teach the New Survival Skills Our Children Need — And What We Can Do About It*. New York: Basic Books, 2008. Print.

The Professional Teacher: Rights and Responsibilities

Anderson, Judith C. *Teacher Professional Autonomy: Balancing Competing Interests*. Harris & Co., 2010. Print.

B.C. School Superintendents' Association. "Assessment and Accountability in Public Education." 2009. Print.

Eagleton, Terry. *After Theory*. London: Allen Lane, 2003. Print.

Labour Relations Code, Section 84 Appointment: Arbitration Award. North Vancouver, B.C.: James Dorsey, 22 Sept. 2009. Print.

School-based Leadership: The Key to Success

"Code of Professional Practice." British Columbia Principals' and Vice Principals' Association. Online.

Fullan, Michael. *Leading in a Culture of Change*. San Francisco: Jossey-Bass, 2001. Print.

Marzano, Robert J., Timothy Waters, and Brian A. McNulty. *School Leadership That Works: From Research to Results*. Alexandria: ASCD, 2005. Print.

Seashore Louis, Karen and Kyla Wahlstrom. "Principals as Cultural Leaders." *Phi Delta Kappan*, Vol. 92, No. 5. Bloomington, In: Phi Delta Kappa International. Feb. 2011. Print.

The Limits of Public Schooling: A Shared Responsibility

Abbott, John, "A Briefing Paper for Parliamentarians on the Design Faults at the Heart of English Education." *The 21st Century Learning Initiative*. August 2009. Online.

Castells, Manuel. *The Rise of the Network Society*. 2nd ed. Malden: Blackwell, 2000. Print.

Dewey, John. *Experience and Education*. 1938. London: Collier, 1963. Print.

Pius G. Ryan, Ed.D., has been involved in public schooling for nineteen years, as a child-care worker, teacher, school psychologist, District Coordinator for Special Education, District Principal of Student Services, Director of Instruction for Diversity and Equity, and Director of Instruction for Education Services. Presently, he is an Assistant Superintendent of the North Vancouver School District.

He also is President-elect of the British Columbia Council of Administrators for Special Education. He sits on the Douglas College Ethics Review Panel, and belongs to the Council for Exceptional Children, the British Columbia Association of School Psychologists, and the British Columbia School Superintendents' Association. He is an acting member of the Provincial Audit Advisory Committee, ESL Provincial Consortium, and Provincial Settlement Workers in Schools Steering Committee, and has served on a number of Ministry of Education review teams.

More recently, he has collaborated on the establishment of an English Language Learner Welcome Centre that provides services to as many as 10,000 new immigrants and refugees annually, assisting them in their transition into Canadian society.

Pius is an accomplished guitarist who has written and recorded original music. He is married and has three children.

Rick K. Ryan, M.Ed., has been involved in public schooling for nineteen years, as a teacher, coach, counsellor, District Resource Counsellor, District Principal of Student Services, and Director of Instruction for Student Support Services. Presently, he is an Assistant Superintendent of the Surrey School District.

He is a member of the British Columbia Council of Administrators for Special Education, the Council for Exceptional Children, and the British Columbia School Superintendents' Association. He has designed and implemented a number of innovative programs in the field of Special Education, including a college-level, paraprofessional training program that enables Applied Behaviour Analysis (ABA) support workers to work effectively with students diagnosed with Autism Spectrum Disorder.

In addition, Rick has developed a comprehensive violence-prevention and intervention program to enhance employee safety in the workplace. He has been consulted nationally concerning school-based violence, threat- and risk-assessment strategies, which are utilized to intervene on behalf of students in emotional crisis.

Prior to his work in education, Rick was selected in the first round of the 1985 Canadian Football League draft by the British Columbia Lions, and played for six seasons. He is married and has three children.

Pius Ryan and Rick Ryan (who are not related) have developed, independently of each other, similar philosophical views concerning public schooling. They believe that "for children, schooling is not only preparation for life — it is life" and that, consequently, district leaders have a responsibility to create systemic structures that improve classroom learning. This goal is accomplished both through leadership and the development of teachers. The authors believe that quality public schooling is established by building aligned, coherent, and sustainable systems and structures that support professional and school development, which, in turn, promote student success.

Pius and Rick may be contacted through their website:

www.edusystems.ca

This site provides contact information, an updated list of speaking engagements, a list of available services, and access to the reference tools that appear in this book, which may be downloaded.